LATEX Notes

Practical Tips for Preparing Technical Documents

J. Kenneth Shultis

Department of Nuclear Engineering
Kansas State University
Manhattan, Kansas

P T R Prentice Hall
Englewood Cliffs, New Jersey 07632

Library of Congress Cataloging-in-Publication Data

Shultis, J. Kenneth
    Latex notes : practical tips for preparing technical documents :
version 1.4 / compiled by J. Kenneth Shultis.
      p. cm.
    Includes bibliographical references and index.
    ISBN 0-13-120973-6
      1. LaTeX (Computer file) 2. Computerized typesetting.
3. Mathematics printing--Data processing. I. Title.
Z253.4.L38S48 1994
686.2'2544--dc20   93-40263
                                        CIP

Editorial/production supervision: *Harriet Tellem*
Cover design: *Lundgren Graphics*
Buyer: *Alexis Heydt*
Acquisitons editor: *Michael Hays*
Editorial assistant: *Kim Intindola*

©1994 P T R Prentice Hall
Prentice-Hall, Inc.
A Paramount Communications Company
Englewood Cliffs, New Jersey 07632

The publisher offers discounts on this book when ordered in bulk quantities.
For more information contact:

    Corporate Sales Department
    P T R Prentice Hall
    113 Sylvan Avenue
    Enlgewood Cliffs, NJ 07632

    Phone: 201-592-2863
    Fax: 201-592-2249

10 9 8 7 6 5 4 3 2 1

ISBN 0-13-120973-6

Prentice-Hall International (UK) Limited, *London*
Prentice-Hall of Australia Pty. Limited, *Sydney*
Prentice-Hall Canada Inc., *Toronto*
Prentice-Hall Hispanoamericana, S.A., *Mexico*
Prentice-Hall of India Private Limited, *New Delhi*
Prentice-Hall of Japan, Inc., *Tokyo*
Simon & Schuster Asia Pte. Ltd., *Singapore*
Editora Prentice-Hall do Brasil, Ltda., *Rio de Janeiro*

Contents

Preface   **ix**

1 Fonts   **1**
  1.1 Special Characters   1
  1.2 Accents and Special Symbols   1
  1.3 Font Sizes   2
  1.4 Font Styles   2
  1.5 Computer Modern Fonts   3
    1.5.1 Changing the Size of a Font   3
    1.5.2 Font Faces and Scaling   4
    1.5.3 Style and Size Availability   4
    1.5.4 Ligatures   5
  1.6 Using Nonstandard Fonts   6
    1.6.1 Specifying a Particular Font Character   6
    1.6.2 Nonstandard Fonts in Math Mode   7
  1.7 Really Large Fonts   8
  1.8 Improvised Special Characters   9
    1.8.1 Symbol for Cents   9
    1.8.2 Blackboard Fonts   9
    1.8.3 Smiley Faces   9
  1.9 The New Font Selection Scheme (NFSS)   10

2 Text Formatting and Lists   **11**
  2.1 Microspacing Adjustments for Text   11
  2.2 Forcing Line Breaks   12
  2.3 Document Line Spacing   12
    2.3.1 Changing Line Spacing in Footnotes   13
  2.4 Hyphenation   13
    2.4.1 Forcing Hyphenation   14
    2.4.2 Forcing a Line Break at a Required Hyphen 14
    2.4.3 Preventing Hyphenation at a Line Break   14

		2.4.4	Turning Hyphenation Off	14
	2.5	Ragged Right		15
		2.5.1	Ragged Right without Hyphenation	15
		2.5.2	Ragged Right with Hyphenation	15
	2.6	Headings		16
		2.6.1	Headings without Numbers	16
		2.6.2	Breaking a Long Heading	16
	2.7	Consistent Underlining		16
	2.8	Vertical and Horizontal Spacing		17
		2.8.1	Variable Space	17
	2.9	Text in Boxes		18
		2.9.1	Right-justifying a Box	19
		2.9.2	Paragraphs with Hanging Indents	20
		2.9.3	A Macro for Indentation	20
		2.9.4	Centering Boxes	21
	2.10	Lists		21
		2.10.1	Itemized List	21
		2.10.2	Enumerated Lists	23
		2.10.3	Lists with Key Words	24
	2.11	Customized Lists		24
		2.11.1	Examples of the List Environment	24
		2.11.2	Creating a New List Environment	26
		2.11.3	Example List Environments	27
	2.12	The Verbatim Environment		28

3 Formatting Pages   **30**
	3.1	Page Layout		30
		3.1.1	Marginal Notes	32
	3.2	Headers and Footers		32
		3.2.1	Head and Foot for the First Page	33
		3.2.2	A Head and Foot Macro	33
		3.2.3	More Elaborate Headers and Footers	34
	3.3	Blank Pages		35
	3.4	Widows and Orphans		35
	3.5	Counters		36
	3.6	Floats		36
		3.6.1	Positioning Floats	37
		3.6.2	Keeping a Group of Tables or Figures Together	37
		3.6.3	Piling up of Floats	38
		3.6.4	Putting Many Floats on a Page	38
	3.7	Two-column Format		39
		3.7.1	Page Layout	39
		3.7.2	Spanning Both Columns	39

3.7.3   Floats in Two-column Format   41
3.7.4   Clearing Pages and Columns   41
3.7.5   Marginal Notes   41

4   Math and Equations   **42**
4.1   Displaying Math Expressions   42
4.2   Composing Math Expressions   42
4.3   Math Spacing Commands   46
4.4   Types of Equations   46
   4.4.1   Simple Equations   46
   4.4.2   Multiconditional Equations   47
   4.4.3   Multiline and Multiple Equations   47
4.5   Equal Spacing in Equations and Eqnarrays   48
4.6   Text in Eqnarray   48
4.7   Vertical Spacing With Struts   49
4.8   Math-mode Font Sizes   50
   4.8.1   Nested Fraction Constructions   50
   4.8.2   Displaystyle in Eqnarrays and Arrays   50
4.9   Manual Equation Numbering   51
4.10   Equations With Left and Right Tags   51
4.11   Multiletter Variables in Math Mode   52
4.12   Roman Font in Math Mode   52
4.13   Boldface in Math Mode   53
   4.13.1   Accents in Boldmath   54
4.14   A Better Dot Product Operator   54
4.15   Two Compound Math Operators   55
4.16   Matrix Expressions   55
4.17   Continued Fractions   56
4.18   Chemical Reaction Arrows   57
4.19   Placing Frames around Equations   57
4.20   Word Equations in Boxes   59
4.21   Math in Section Titles   59

5   Tables   **60**
5.1   Types of Tables   60
   5.1.1   Captions and Reference Labels   61
5.2   The `tabbing` Environment   61
   5.2.1   An Instructional Example   62
5.3   The `tabular` Environment   64
   5.3.1   Aligning Numbers on the Decimal Point   67
   5.3.2   Vertical Alignment of Tables Headings   67
   5.3.3   A Simple Floating Table Example   68
   5.3.4   Tables in a Minipage   69

5.3.5	Side-by-Side Tables	71
5.3.6	Vertical Alignment of Column Entries	72
5.3.7	Paragraphs in a Box	73
5.3.8	Controlling Spacing in Tables	73
5.4	TABLE Macros	74
5.4.1	Using the TABLE Macros	75

6 Graphics   **80**

6.1	Methods for Including Graphics	80
6.1.1	Cut and Paste	80
6.1.2	Use the `picture` Environment	81
6.1.3	Extend LaTeX's `picture` Capabilities	81
6.1.4	Use Other Programs to Generate LaTeX Pictures	82
6.1.5	Use Non-LaTeX Graphics	82
6.2	The Picture Environment	83
6.2.1	Summary of Picture Commands	84
6.2.2	Reusing Picture Elements	88
6.3	Extending the `picture` Environment	89
6.4	Programs to Generate LaTeX Pictures	90
6.4.1	A GNUPLOT Example	90
6.5	Using Non-LaTeX Graphics	92
6.5.1	Importing PCL Graphics Files	92
6.5.2	Importing PostScript Graphic Files	98
6.6	Producing Graphic Files for LaTeX	103
6.6.1	Converting from HPGL Format	103
6.6.2	More General Graphic Conversion Programs	103
6.6.3	Creating PostScript Graphics with PSTricks	104

7 Large Documents   **105**

7.1	The Root File	105
7.2	Macros in the Preamble	107
7.3	Loading Style Files	108
7.4	Front Matter	108
7.4.1	Title Page	109
7.4.2	Preface	109
7.4.3	Table of Contents	109
7.4.4	Lists of Figures and Tables	110
7.4.5	Adding Entries to Contents, Tables, and Figures Lists	110
7.4.6	Roman Page Numbering for Front Matter	111
7.4.7	Reformatting the Table of Contents	111
7.5	Excluding Part of the Input	112
7.6	Footnotes	112
7.6.1	Footnotes in a Heading	112

7.6.2	Changing the Footnote Symbol	113
7.6.3	Footnotes inside Boxes	113
7.7	Cross References	113
7.8	Citations and Bibliography	114
7.8.1	The Bibliography List	114
7.8.2	Making References in the Text	115
7.8.3	Printing the Bibliography	115
7.8.4	Citation Variations	115
7.9	References and Citations in Captions	115
7.10	Making an Index	116
7.10.1	Doing It Yourself	117
7.10.2	The MAKEINDEX Program	118

8 Useful Styles   **120**

8.1	Finding and Obtaining Style Files	120
8.1.1	Where to Find Style Files	121
8.2	Verbatim Text from an External File	121
8.3	Captions with Hanging Indents	122
8.4	More Flexible Numbering of Equations	123
8.4.1	A Corrected `eqnarray` Environment	124
8.4.2	The `eqalign` Environment	124
8.4.3	The `eqalignno` Environment	124
8.4.4	The `eqaligntwo` Environment	125
8.4.5	The `cases` Environment	125
8.4.6	The `subequations` Environment	125
8.5	Wrapping Text around a Figure: I	126
8.6	Wrapping Text around a Figure: II	127
8.7	Customizing Headers and Footers	129
8.7.1	Simple Use	129
8.7.2	Rules in Header and Footer	130
8.7.3	Headers and Footers Wider Than the Text	130
8.7.4	Multiline Headers and Footers	130
8.7.5	Headers and Footers for Even and Odd Pages	130
8.7.6	Separate Headers and Footers for Chapter Pages	131
8.7.7	Defaults	131
8.7.8	Section Titles in the Headers and Footers	131
8.8	Frames and Boxes	133
8.8.1	Fancy Boxes	133
8.8.2	Large Frames	134
8.9	Multicolumns of Text	135
8.9.1	The User Interface	135
8.9.2	Balancing Columns	136
8.9.3	Floats	137

| | 8.9.4 | Warnings | 137 |

9   Macros and Miscellaneous Tricks   138

9.1	Basics of Macro Programming	139
	9.1.1 Defining New Commands	139
	9.1.2 Some Commands Used in Macros	141
9.2	Page Layout Tricks	142
	9.2.1 Macro for Side-by-Side Displays	142
	9.2.2 Underlining and Striking out Text	143
	9.2.3 San Serif Section Headings	144
	9.2.4 Outdenting Headings	145
	9.2.5 Right Headers to Reference Last Section	146
	9.2.6 New Environment for Indentation of Text	146
9.3	Changing the Caption Format	147
	9.3.1 Changing the Caption Font Size and Width	147
	9.3.2 Changing the Style of the Caption Label	148
	9.3.3 Changing *Figure* to *Fig.*	149
9.4	Numbering Things	150
	9.4.1 Page Numbering with "chapter-page"	150
	9.4.2 Page Numbers to the Right of Text	151
	9.4.3 Numbering Equations as "(Section.Equation)"	151
9.5	Equation Tricks	152
	9.5.1 Dashed Lines in Arrays and Tabulars	152
	9.5.2 Equal Spacing in Equations and Eqnarrays	152
	9.5.3 Math Macro for Over- and UnderBrackets	153
9.6	References, Bibliographies, and Endnotes	155
	9.6.1 Superscripts for References	155
	9.6.2 Line Breaks for Long Citations	155
	9.6.3 Bibliographies at Chapter Ends	155
	9.6.4 Macro for Endnotes	156

Appendix A: Symbols Available in Math Mode   159

Appendix B: Format Parameters   163

Index   171

Preface

A few years ago I discovered TEXand was immediately fascinated by its ability to produce beautifully typeset technical and scientific documents. More attractive still was the superset of TEX called LATEX which frees the user from much of the mundane chores required by TEX. The basic philosophy of LATEX is to free the writer from details of formatting, equation numbering, and the like, and allow him or her to concentrate on the document content. An excellent concept.

Unfortunately, a LATEX apprentice soon desires to step outside the strictures imposed by LATEX. Yet the road to becoming a TEX wizard is long and arduous, and, for most of us, there is not enough time to travel it. Rather, most LATEX users simply wish to find a quick fix to make some minor change in the way LATEX wants to do something. If you happen to live among friendly TEX wizards, you are fortunate; finding a fix then is often simply a matter of seeking an indulgence from a wizard. For those without such resources and who do not wish to undertake the studies, trials, and initiation rites to TEX wizardry, trying to cajole LATEX into doing things your way is often a frustrating experience. The refrain "I know it can be done, but I don't know how" is often muttered.

TEX, from which LATEX is built, is a rich programming language and it is not surprising that many different solutions to a given problem can be found. For example, suppose you want to use a normal text hyphen in place of the longer minus sign in complex math formulas and also have it change size in superscripts and subscripts. As D. Hosek observes, your solution depends on the type of TEX person you are.

- A TEX user would use: `\hbox{-}`
- A LATEX user would use: `\mbox{-}`
- A TEXpert would use: `{\rm-}`
  (It doesn't work but TEXpert is a bogus term anyway.)
- A TEXnician would use: `\mathchar"002D`

- A TEX hacker would use:
  `\mathchoice{\hbox{-}}{\hbox{-}}{\hbox{\sevenrm-}}{\hbox{\fiverm-}}`

- And a TEX wizard would use: `\mathchar28717`
  (Why make the simple answer appear less than magical?)

These notes began as learning exercises and reference sheets as I attempted to understand LATEX. Although Leslie Lamport's definitive reference *LATEX: User's Guide and Reference Manual* is a very complete (if sometimes terse) description of LATEX, I often found it hard to find what I needed to know or to separate what was important to me from other esoteric features of LATEX. Thus my set of notes. Initially, they were just lists of things I had a hard time remembering but that I used regularly and that I could quickly find in my notes when needed. However, I soon started adding recipes and tricks as I struggled to extend LATEX or to understand some mysterious part of Lamport's scripture.

The recipes and tricks included in these notes have been gleaned from many sources, including a few home grown efforts. The solutions may not always be the most elegant; rather, they represent tricks found to solve various formatting problems encountered during my initial efforts in using LATEX to prepare scientific documents. As such, these notes are also a personal diary of my frustrations with trying to understand Lamport's brief explanations and with prodding LATEX to go beyond its original capabilities. They also represent the joys I experienced as I forced LATEX to my will. Finally, no attempt at completeness is made; the topics represent only a small part of what can be done with LATEX. The contents reflect those parts of LATEX that I have found most helpful while preparing technical documents.

In the hope that other beginners will have fewer struggles and greater pleasures as they mature to competent LATEX users, I offer these notes as a guide to those who have mastered the basics of LATEX and who are now ready to venture off the main LATEX highway to explore some of the less traveled paths afforded by this powerful typesetting program.

Before Using This Book

This book is based on the premise that its readers are both acquainted with the basics of LATEX and know how to run LATEX on their computer systems. If you have never used LATEX, you will find either one of the following publications will provide a good introduction to LATEX.

J. Hahn, *LATEX for Everyone*, Prentice Hall, New York, NY, 1991.

G. Maltby, *An Introduction to TEX and Friends*, freely available from TEX archives on the Internet (see Section 8.1.1).

Finally, no matter what level of LaTeX user you are, a copy of one of the following comprehensive books is an indispensable reference work to have at your side as you prepare LaTeX documents.

L. Lamport, *LaTeX: A Document Preparation System*, Addison-Wesley, New York, NY, 1986.

A. Johnstone, *LaTeX Concisely*, Prentice Hall, New York, NY 1992.

Acknowledgments

During the drafting of this book, I received help and suggestions from many of my colleagues and students at Kansas State University. To N. Dean Eckhoff, I extend special thanks for introducing me a few years ago to TeX and for sharing with me an initiate's enthusiasm as we began to explore the capabilities of LaTeX. Dick Faw and Ken Carpenter unselfishly gave me help with many LaTeX problems, and for their many useful suggestions I am deeply appreciative. Finally, this book would not have been possible without the many contributors to the news group `comp.text.tex` on Internet from whom I have learned much and whose ideas and suggestions are reflected in many parts of this work. For the help from this vast pool of experts, I am especially grateful.

JKS
Kansas State University

Chapter 1

Fonts

1.1 Special Characters

All the keyboard characters, except for ten characters that are used for special purposes, can be typed in directly. The nine special characters $ & % # _ { } ~ and ^ are produced by

$	\$	&	\&	%	\%
{	\{	}	\}	_	_
#	\#	^	\^{}	~	\~{}

The tenth character \ can be produced with `$\backslash$`.

1.2 Accents and Special Symbols

The following commands sequences are used to produce accented letters, foreign characters, and a few special symbols. These commands are used in the normal text mode.

ò	\`{o}	õ	\~{o}	ǒ	\v{o}	ǫ	\c{o}
ó	\'{o}	ō	\={o}	ő	\H{o}	ǫ	\d{o}
ô	\^{o}	ȯ	\.{o}	ȯȯ	\t{oo}	ǫ	\b{o}
ö	\"{o}	ŏ	\u{o}	ø	\o	Ø	\O
å	\aa	œ	\oe	æ	\ae	ß	\ss
Å	\AA	Œ	\OE	Æ	\AE		
ı	\i	ȷ	\j	ł	\l	Ł	\L
¿	?`	¡	!`	†	\dag	‡	\ddag
©	\copyright	§	\S	¶	\P	£	\pounds

1

LATEX also has a great many symbols that can be used in math mode. Rather than list them all here, a complete listing of these symbols is given in Appendix A.

1.3   Font Sizes

LATEX has several sizes of fonts that can be invoked by the {*sizecmd* text...} construct. The font-size commands (*sizecmd*) and the size of fonts they produce are listed below. The three options in this table refer to the default font size specified for the document as a style option in the \documentstyle command.

Command	Example	10 pt option	11 pt option	12 pt option
\tiny	5 Point Font	5 pt	6 pt	6 pt
\scriptsize	7 Point Font	7 pt	8 pt	8 pt
\footnotesize	8 Point Font	8 pt	9 pt	10 pt
\small	9 Point Font	9 pt	10 pt	11 pt
\normalsize	10 Point Font	10 pt	11 pt	12 pt
\large	12 Point	12 pt	12 pt	14 pt
\Large	14 Point	14 pt	14 pt	17 pt
\LARGE	17 Point	17 pt	17 pt	20 pt
\huge	20 Pt	20 pt	20 pt	25 pt
\Huge	25 Pt	25 pt	25 pt	25 pt

1.4   Font Styles

Standard LATEX has available the following font styles (shown in 10-point size). Notice that the last four styles are used only in math mode.

Example	Command
Roman (computer modern)	{\rm Roman (computer modern)}
Bold Roman	{\bf Bold Roman}
Sans Serif Typestyle	{\sf Sans Serif Typestyle}
SMALL CAPITALS	{\sc small capitals}
Typewrite Style	{\tt Typewrite Style}
Slanted Typestyle	{\sl Slanted Typestyle}
Italics Typestyle	{\it Italics Typestyle}
Math Italics Typestyle	$Math\ Italics\ Typestyle$
Bold Math Italics	{\boldmath $Bold\ Math\ Italics$}
CALLIGRAPHIC	$\cal CALLIGRAPHIC$
BOLD CALLIGRAPHIC	{\boldmath $\cal BOLD\ CALLIGRAPHIC$}

1.5 Computer Modern Fonts

The standard font style used by LaTeX is computer modern. A standard set of 75 different font face styles is usually installed and can be made available to LaTeX. However, generally not all these styles are known to LaTeX. In the file `lfonts.tex`, which is used by TeX to make an executable version of LaTeX, many font definitions will be found commented out because of the limited internal memory possessed by most versions of TeX. In the following table the names of the 10-point computer modern fonts that are in the standard 75-font set are listed. Those fonts not normally defined for LaTeX are indicated by an asterisk (*).

Font	Style	Font	Style
cmr10	roman	cmitt10*	italic typewriter
cmmi10	math italic	cmsltt10*	slanted typewriter
cmmib10*	bold math italic	cmss10	sans serif
cmsy10	math symbols	cmssi10*	italic sans serif
cmbsy10*	bold symbols	cmssbx10*	bold sans serif
cmti10	text italic	cmcsc10*	small caps
cmsl10	slanted	lasy10	LaTeX symbols
cmbx10	extended bold	lasyb10*	bold LaTeX symbols
cmbxsl10*	extended bold slanted	cmu10*	unslanted italic
cmtt10	typewriter		

However, as long as an undefined font is available, it can still be used in a document. For a particular font to be available, its metric `.TFM` file (which defines each character's size) and its bit-mapped `.PK` file (use by the DVI drivers for screen previewing and printing) must be where LaTeX can find them. If the nondefined font is available, first use the `\newfont` command to define a font command for it. For example, suppose you want to use 10-point italic sans serif (font `cmssi10`). First place in the preamble or document the statement `\newfont{\ISS}{cmssi10}` to define `\ISS` as the font change command for this font style. Then the sequence `{\ISS Italic Sans Serif}` will produce *Italic Sans Serif*.

1.5.1 Changing the Size of a Font

In LaTeX the `\newfont` command can also be used to define a new font command that magnifies or scales a specific font. For example, suppose you want to define the font command `\BSS` (Big Sans Serif) to refer to 10-point sans serif expanded to a height of 17 points, place the following statement in your document

```
\newfont{\BSS}{cmss10 scaled\magstep3}
```

The optional parameter `scaled\magstep3` indicates that the 10-point `cmss10` font (computer modern, sans serif, 10 point) is to be magnified or scaled by a factor of $1.2^3 \simeq 1.728$. Then in your document the sequence `{\BBS BigSS}` will produce **BigSS**, which is 17 points high.

The six allowed values of `\magstep` and their magnification factors are:

`\magstephalf`	$1.2^{0.5}$	$\simeq 1.095$
`\magstep1`	1.2^1	$\simeq 1.200$
`\magstep2`	1.2^2	$\simeq 1.440$
`\magstep3`	1.2^3	$\simeq 1.728$
`\magstep4`	1.2^4	$\simeq 2.074$
`\magstep5`	1.2^5	$\simeq 2.488$

Be aware that not all font styles are usually available in all `\magstep` sizes. The less frequently used 10-point font styles, for example, are usually available only in the lower two `\magstep`s.

1.5.2   Font Faces and Scaling

Most characters in a particular font family change slightly in shape and density as the font size is adjusted. Scaling a font does *not* preserve these design differences. For instance, the computer modern roman font `cmr10` scaled to 17 points (`\magstep` 3) is slightly different from the true 17-point computer modern font (`cmr17`) as can be seen in the following example:

abcde ABCDE 12345   `cmr10` scaled to 17 points

abcde ABCDE 12345   `cmr17`

Notice that the scaled font has heavier and wider characters, which are also shaped slightly differently than the corresponding 17-point characters. Generally, you should use the font designed for the specified character height. Unfortunately, not all LaTeX fonts are available in all sizes, and when you need to use a particular font size that is unavailable then defining a scaled version of the font allows you to approximate the needed font.

1.5.3   Style and Size Availability

Not all font styles are available in all font sizes. Each style and size combination requires its own font file (`.PK` and `.TFM` files). Some are *preloaded* when LaTeX is started, others are only *loaded on demand* to reduce memory requirements, and others are *unavailable*. In normal text mode, loaded and loaded-on-demand fonts behave the same. If a particular font style of some unusual size is not available, LaTeX will generally substitute the font of closest size and issue a warning message. The available font style and size combinations depend on your particular LaTeX implementation (see your *local guide*). Table 1.1 shows the font style and size availability for a typical implementation (in this case PCTeX).

In normal text (paragraph and LR modes), loaded and loaded-on-demand fonts behave the same. In math mode they do not; only preloaded fonts may be used. Loaded fonts will be substituted, often without warning, for unavailable or load-on-demand fonts used in math expressions. To use load-on-demand fonts in math mode, you must first load them with the \load command. Here is an example in 8-point type for which the sans serif style is not preloaded.

The variable MVB$_a$ is...

The variable MVB$_a$ is...

```
\footnotesize   %-- 8 pt size in 10pt doc
The variable ${\sf MVB_{a}}$ is...\\
\load{\footnotesize}{\sf}  %--load 8pt SS
The variable ${\sf MVB_{a}}$ is...
```

Table 1.1: Typical availability of LaTeX font styles

	\it	\bf	\sl	\sf	\sc	\tt	\rm	\mit
5 pt	D	D	X	X	X	X	P	P
6 pt	X	D	X	X	X	X	P	P
7 pt	P	D	X	X	X	X	P	P
8 pt	P	D	D	D	D	D	P	P
9 pt	P	P	D	D	D	P	P	P
10 pt	P	P	P	P	D	P	P	P
11 pt	P	P	P	P	D	P	P	P
12 pt	P	P	P	P	D	P	P	P
14 pt	D	P	D	D	D	D	P	P
17 pt	D	P	D	D	D	D	P	P
20 pt	D	D	D	D	D	D	P	P
25 pt	X	D	X	X	X	X	P	P

X = unavailable, P = preloaded, D = loaded on demand

1.5.4 Ligatures

Ligatures such as ff fi fl ffl ffi or *ff fi fl ffl ffi* are performed automatically by LaTeX. However, on rare occasions you may wish to suppress a ligature. For example, the word "shelfful" without a ligature looks better than "shelfful" with a ligature. To suppress the ligature, use shelf{}ful.

1.6   Using Nonstandard Fonts

LaTeX can use virtually any font once appropriate font files have been created. For this reason, LaTeX is widely used to prepare many foreign language documents.

To use a particular nonstandard font (one that is not part of LaTeX), the metric .TFM file (which defines each character's size) and the bit-mapped .PK file (used by DVI drivers for screen previewing and printing) for the font set must first be obtained and made available to LaTeX. Then the \newfont command is used in the document preamble to define a command name for specifying the use of the fonts. For example, in the preamble you might use

```
\newfont{\Fr}{eufm10}   %-- Fraktur, medium face
\newfont{\Sc}{eusm10}   %-- Script, medium face
\newfont{\Bb}{msbm10}   %-- Blackboard, med. face
```

to define \Fr, \Sc, and \Bb as special font commands. (The font files EUFN10.PK, EUSM10.PK, and MSBM10.PK and their corresponding .TFM files are part of $\mathcal{AMS}$-LaTeX.) To produce a scaled 12-point version of the Fraktur font use

```
\newfont{\Fr}{eufm10 scaled\magstep1}   %-- 12pt Fraktur
```

To use the Fraktur (German) font in the normal text mode of LaTeX, simply invoke {\Fr ....} to place the text between the braces in Fraktur font. For example, {\Fr ABC...XYZ}, {\Sc ABC...XYZ}, and {\Bb ABC...XYZ} produce

$$\mathfrak{ABCDEFGHIJKLMNOPQRSTUVWXYZ}$$
$$\mathscr{ABCDEFGHIJKLMNOPQRSTUVWXYZ}$$
$$\mathbb{ABCDEFGHIJKLMNOPQRSTUVWXYZ}$$

1.6.1   Specifying a Particular Font Character

A LaTeX font set contains 128 characters, many of which are not alphabetic characters and cannot be represented by a keyboard symbol. To use these characters in your document, the \symbol command is used. For example, $\mathscr{R}$ is character 82 in EUSM10 and can be referred to as either {\Sc R} or {\Sc \symbol{82}}. Some symbols, such as $\frown$, can be invoked only with the \symbol command, as in this case with {\Bb \symbol{121}}.

To find the decimal number of a particular character in a font file, it is necessary to obtain a listing of the characters with their numbers. Such a font character listing is often presented in a table similar to that of Table 1.2.

Table 1.2: Example decimal character table for the blackboard font set `msbm10`

	$x{=}0$	1	2	3	4	5	6	7	8	9
x	$\lneqq$	$\gneqq$	$\nleq$	$\ngeq$	$\nleqslant$	$\ngeqslant$	$\lneq$	$\gneq$	$\lneqq$	$\gneqq$
$1x$	$\nless$	$\ngtr$	$\lnsim$	$\gnsim$	$\lnapprox$	$\gnapprox$	$\precnsim$	$\succnsim$	$\precnapprox$	$\succnapprox$
$2x$	$\subsetneqq$	$\supsetneqq$	$\precneqq$	$\succneqq$	$\precnapprox$	$\succnapprox$	$\lnapprox$	$\gnapprox$	$\sim$	$\neq$
$3x$	$/$	$\backslash$	$\subsetneq$	$\supsetneq$	$\nsubseteq$	$\nsupseteq$	$\subsetneqq$	$\supsetneqq$	$\varsubsetneq$	$\varsupsetneq$
$4x$	$\subsetneq$	$\supsetneq$	$\nsubseteq$	$\nsupseteq$	$\nparallel$	$\dagger$	$\prime$	$\nshortmid$	$\nvdash$	$\nVdash$
$5x$	$\nvDash$	$\nVDash$	$\ntrianglelefteq$	$\ntrianglerighteq$	$\ntriangleleft$	$\ntriangleright$	$\nleftarrow$	$\nrightarrow$	$\nLeftarrow$	$\nRightarrow$
$6x$	$\nleftrightarrow$	$\nLeftrightarrow$	$\divideontimes$	$\varnothing$	$\nexists$	$\mathbb{A}$	$\mathbb{B}$	$\mathbb{C}$	$\mathbb{D}$	$\mathbb{E}$
$7x$	$\mathbb{F}$	$\mathbb{G}$	$\mathbb{H}$	$\mathbb{I}$	$\mathbb{J}$	$\mathbb{K}$	$\mathbb{L}$	$\mathbb{M}$	$\mathbb{N}$	$\mathbb{O}$
$8x$	$\mathbb{P}$	$\mathbb{Q}$	$\mathbb{R}$	$\mathbb{S}$	$\mathbb{T}$	$\mathbb{U}$	$\mathbb{V}$	$\mathbb{W}$	$\mathbb{X}$	$\mathbb{Y}$
$9x$	$\mathbb{Z}$	$\frown$	$\frown$	$\frown$	$\frown$		$\Finv$	$\Game$		
$10x$		$\mho$	$\eth$	$\eqsim$	$\beth$	$\gimel$	$\daleth$	$<$	$>$	
$11x$	$\ltimes$	$\rtimes$	$\restriction$	$\Vvdash$	$\diagdown$	$\thicksim$	$\thickapprox$	$\approxeq$	$\succapprox$	$\precapprox$
$12x$	$\curvearrowleft$	$\curvearrowright$	$\digamma$	$\varkappa$	$\Bbbk$	$\hslash$	$\hbar$	$\backepsilon$		

1.6.2 Nonstandard Fonts in Math Mode

The new font commands \Fr, \Sc, and \Bb *cannot* be used in math mode. You must place these fonts in an \mbox if they are to be used in a formula. For example, to produce $\mathcal{E} = \mathcal{D} \times \mathcal{R}$, you must use

$\mbox{\Sc E} = \mbox{\Sc D} \times \mbox{\Sc R}$.

The TEX command \def can be used to define a shorthand command to print a particular character from a nonstandard font set when in math mode. For example, first place in the preamble the sequences

```
\def\ScE{\mbox{\Sc \symbol{69}}}     %-- script E
\def\ScD{\mbox{\Sc \symbol{68}}}     %-- script D
\def\ScR{\mbox{\Sc \symbol{82}}}     %-- script R
```

so that $\mathcal{E} = \mathcal{D} \times \mathcal{R}$ can be entered more compactly as $\ScE = \ScD \times \ScR$.

1.7   Really Large Fonts

The standard font collection used by LaTeX also has a large 1-inch font, `cminch`, that can be used by defining in the preamble the font commands

```
\newfont{\BIG}{cminch}                    %--- One-inch font
\newfont{\sqBIG}{cminch scaled 833}  %--- squashed 1-in font
```

Note, this font cannot be magnified, although its interletter spacing can be decreased by scaling it to less than the normal size of 1000 (see the previous definition of `\sqBIG`). Here are three examples with different spacing between letters. These examples were produced with the commands `{\sqBIG HUGE}`, `{\BIG HUGE}`, and, to increase the normal interletter spacing, `{\BIG H\hfil U\hfil G\hfil E}`.

HUGE

HUGE

HUGE

1.8   Improvised Special Characters

Sometimes the standard fonts available to LaTeX will not contain some special character that you need. Although the best solution is to use METAFONT(a font generation program) to generate a special font set that contains the needed character, you can often approximate the character by superimposing several existing characters and/or line rules. Here are three examples

1.8.1   Symbol for Cents

One symbol missing from LaTeX's font sets is the symbol for cents. Here are four commands that approximate this symbol:

```
\newcommand{\centa}{{\sf c}\!\!|}      %-- suggested by D.E. Knuth
\newcommand{\centb}{\hbox{\rm\rlap/c}}
\newcommand{\centc}{\mbox{\small \rm c}\!\!\!\!\;\scriptstyle /}
\newcommand{\centd}{\mbox{\small \sf c}\!\!\!\!\;\scriptstyle /}
```

Here are the results of these different attempts. None is perfect.

$$85\$\backslash\texttt{centa}\$ \text{ produces } 85\cent$$
$$85\$\backslash\texttt{centb}\$ \text{ produces } 85\cent$$
$$85\$\backslash\texttt{centc}\$ \text{ produces } 85\cent$$
$$85\$\backslash\texttt{centd}\$ \text{ produces } 85\cent$$

1.8.2   Blackboard Fonts

The following commands in the preamble will allow you to use a poor man's approximation to blackboard fonts.

```
\newcommand{\BBR}{{\sf R\hspace*{-0.9ex}\rule{0.15ex}{1.5ex}\hspace*{0.9ex}}}
\newcommand{\BBN}{{\sf N\hspace*{-1.0ex}\rule{0.15ex}{1.3ex}\hspace*{1.0ex}}}
\newcommand{\BBQ}{{\sf Q\hspace*{-1.1ex}\rule{0.15ex}{1.5ex}\hspace*{1.1ex}}}
\newcommand{\BBC}{{\sf C\hspace*{-0.9ex}\rule{0.15ex}{1.3ex}\hspace*{0.9ex}}}
\newcommand{\BBD}{{\sf D\hspace*{-0.9ex}\rule{0.15ex}{1.5ex}\hspace*{0.9ex}}}
```

Thus, to produce ℝ ℕ ℚ ℂ 𝔻, enter \BBR \BBN \BBQ \BBC \BBD.

1.8.3   Smiley Faces

Just for fun, here are three faces: \smiley ☺   \blahey ☺   \frowney ☹

The 10-point macros for \smiley, \frowney, and \blahey are as follows (for 11-point and 12-point documents, some tweaking of the dimensions is needed).

```
%-- Smiley Face
\def\smiley{\hbox{\large$\bigcirc$\hspace{-.80em}%
\raise.2ex\hbox{$\cdot\cdot$}\kern-.61em     %--- .56
\lower.2ex\hbox{\scriptsize$\smile$}}\ }

%-- Frowney Face
\def\frowney{\hbox{\large$\bigcirc$\hspace{-.80em}%
\raise.2ex\hbox{$\cdot\cdot$}\kern-.635em
\lower.2ex\hbox{\scriptsize$\frown$}}\ }

%-- Blahey Face
\def\blahey{\hbox{\large$\bigcirc$\hspace{-.80em}%
\raise.2ex\hbox{$\cdot\cdot$}\kern-.46em
\lower.3ex\hbox{\scriptsize\hbox{--}}}\ }
```

1.9   The New Font Selection Scheme (NFSS)

The discussion in this chapter about using different fonts is based on the original font selection scheme described in Lamport's book. In the late 1980s, LaTeX wizards Frank Mittelbach and Rainer Schöpf devised an alternative and improved scheme for using fonts with LaTeX (as well as with TeX and $\mathcal{AMS}$-LaTeX). This new font selection scheme (NFSS) lets you use all the standard fonts (that is, those that come with LaTeX) and nonstandard fonts in both text *and* math modes without having to preload all the fonts (and thereby consume useful memory).

The NFSS also allows you to use the old font selection scheme to ensure backward compatibility. Moreover, it is the only practical way of using $\mathcal{AMS}$-LaTeX fonts and postscript fonts with LaTeX. This new scheme will eventually become a standard part of LaTeX in future releases, although many implementations of LaTeX have already been modified to use the NFSS.

Chapter 2

Text Formatting and Lists

2.1   Microspacing Adjustments for Text

LaTeX is usually pretty good at figuring out the spacing between words. However, there are some special cases where you must help.

After Punctuation: The command `\␣` (where ␣ represents a space) produces normal interword spacing, and `\@` indicates normal intersentence spacing. LaTeX always assumes that . ends a sentence *unless* it immediately follows an uppercase letter. In this case, LaTeX assumes that the period is part of an abbreviation and not a sentence ending. Here are some examples.

Smith et al. used plan B. So did we.	`Smith et al.\ used plan B\@. So did we.`
Smith et al. used plan B. So did we.	`Smith et al. used plan B. So did we.`
Gases (argon, etc.) are found...	`Gases (argon, etc.)\ are found...`
Gases (argon, etc.) are found...	`Gases (argon, etc.) are found...`
"...e.g. blood of type O." Thus...	`` ``...e.g.\ blood of type O\@." Thus... ``
"...e.g. blood of type O." Thus...	`` ``...e.g. blood of type O." Thus... ``

Extra Space: The command `\,` is used to provide a small extra space where LaTeX would not normally put one, for example, to separate adjacent quotation marks. A special spacing command `\/` is used to insert extra space between italics and roman characters and does nothing if it follows a roman letter. Here are some examples.

He said "'wine' or 'beer'".	`` He said ``\,`wine' or 'beer'\,". ``
He said "'wine' or 'beer'".	`` He said ```wine' or 'beer'". ``
He *did*n't do it.	`He {\em did}\/n't do it.`
He *did*n't do it.	`He {\em did}n't do it.`
dis*till*ate	`dis\/{\em till}\/ate`
dis*till*ate	`dis{\em till}ate`

11

Lock Space: Normally a space indicates a separation between words and is a place where LaTeX may break a line. However, sometimes you may wish to prevent a space being used as a line break. To avoid a bad line break, simply "lock" the two words together with ~ as in `D.~Knuth` or `Fig.~3`. Notice that the lock space character ~ also prevents the . in `Fig.` being treated as the end of a sentence.

2.2   Forcing Line Breaks

To make LaTeX break a line of text use the `\newline` command or its shorthand equivalent `\\`. The resulting broken line will be left justified, leaving a ragged right. The `\\*` form of the line break command inhibits page breaking between the broken line and the following line. Both the `\\` and `\\*` commands take an optional argument to increase (or decrease) the normal interline spacing following a broken line. Thus `\\[.25in]` inserts a quarter-inch vertical space after the forced line break.

LaTeX is very fussy about breaking lines. For an overfilled line, you can suggest where a line break should be (while still maintaining right justification) by placing `\linebreak[n]` at the desired break point. The integer n is in the range from 1 to 4, 1 being the mildest suggestion to LaTeX and 4 being compulsory. Similarly, the `\nolinebreak[n]` inhibits a line break.

When many bad line breaks occur (for example, after turning off hyphenation in a narrow column of text), invoking the `\sloppy` command will allow LaTeX to use more interword space to avoid bad line breaks. The command `\fussy` returns LaTeX to its normal word spacing standards.

2.3   Document Line Spacing

Typeset documents should be single spaced. However, extra space between text lines is sometimes needed, such as in draft manuscripts or to meet requirements imposed by others. The line spacing for a LaTeX document is, by default, single space. To change to space and a half, for example, include the following line in the document preamble.

```
\renewcommand{\baselinestretch}{1.5}
```

Sometimes in a nonsingle-spaced document, you will want to return temporarily to single spacing (for example, for quoted material or captions in figures and tables). To do this while maintaining the same font size (here `\normalsize`), insert the following line just before the portion of the text that you want to be put into single space.

```
\renewcommand{\baselinestretch}{1} \tiny   \normalsize
```

To return to space and a half, set the `\baselinestretch` to a value of 1.5 using the previous construction. The double change of font size is needed to force LaTeX to make the line spacing change even though the size of the font is not being changed.

If you are going to switch frequently between single space and space and a half, place the following two macros in the preamble of your document.

```
\newcommand{\DS}{\renewcommand{\baselinestretch}{1.5}
                 \tiny \normalsize }
\newcommand{\SS}{\renewcommand{\baselinestretch}{1}
                 \tiny \normalsize }
```

The new command `\DS` will then cause the current paragraph and all subsequent text output to have space and a half line spacing. The command `\SS` likewise will cause LaTeX to begin using single line spacing.

2.3.1   Changing Line Spacing in Footnotes

To force a footnote to have single spacing in a double-spaced document, you do not need the double font-size change since the footnote automatically undergoes a font-size change. Thus, you can enter

```
he saw an elephant%
    \renewcommand{\baselinestretch}{1}\footnote{a rather large
    mammal}\renewcommand{\baselinestretch}{2}
and many gnus during his travels.
```

Again a simple macro can make this awkward construction much easier. In the preamble, define the following new command.

```
\newcommand{\SSfootnote}[1]{\renewcommand{\baselinestretch}{1}%
        \footnote{#1}\renewcommand{\baselinestretch}{2}}
```

Then the above example could be written more easily as

```
he saw an elephant\SSfootnote{a rather large mammal} and many ...
```

2.4   Hyphenation

LaTeX by default uses right justification and automatic word hyphenation to produce good line breaks for a paragraph. On rare occasions you may have to intervene and help with the hyphenation. Here are some tricks.

2.4.1 Forcing Hyphenation

Although LaTeX almost never hyphenates incorrectly, it does sometimes miss spots in a word where a hyphen could go. This is particularly true of foreign words. You can suggest hyphenation points in such a word by using `\-` in the word, for example, `brems\-strahl\-ung`. If troublesome words are to be used often in a document, you can tell LaTeX their hyphenation for every occurrence with the `\hyphenation` command. For example, to tell LaTeX the hyphenation of the words "bremsstrahlung" and "phlogiston," put the following statement in the preamble:

```
\hyphenation{brems-strahl-ung  phlo-gis-ton}
```

2.4.2 Forcing a Line Break at a Required Hyphen

If you encounter a hyphenated word such as "radiation-induced" and you want to break the line at the hyphen, do not use `\--` since this will give you two hyphens. The trick is to specify `\radiation-\linebreak[1]induced`.

2.4.3 Preventing Hyphenation at a Line Break

To prevent LaTeX from hyphenating a particular word at a line break, place the word in an `\mbox{}`, for example `\mbox{bremsstrahlung}`.

2.4.4 Turning Hyphenation Off

Sometimes you may wish to avoid hyphenating words at the end of all lines. One method to turn off hyphenation while preserving right justification is to set the hyphenation penalties to very large values by placing in the preamble

```
\hyphenpenalty=10000  \exhyphenpenalty=10000
```

Although this approach will usually produce right-justified lines, some lines may become too long because of large words near the line breaks. These bad line breaks can be ameliorated somewhat by issuing the `\sloppy` command to allow LaTeX to use more than the normal interword spacing.

2.5   Ragged Right

Normally a typeset document should have the lines right justified. This is the default for LaTeX. However, there may be reasons you want to avoid right justification.

2.5.1   Ragged Right without Hyphenation

Occasionally, you may want to turn off both the hyphenation for a document (or part of a document) and also the right justification of the lines. For example, some journals actually require manuscripts to have this format. To do this in LaTeX, embed the text in the `flushleft` environment, that is, between the commands `\begin{flushleft}` ... `\end{flushleft}`. This will turn off hyphenation and produce lines with ragged right margins as in this paragraph. Also this procedure appears to set the `\parindent` to zero, but you may reset it with `\setlength{\parindent}{.25in}`.

2.5.2   Ragged Right with Hyphenation

Some manuscripts are required by publishers to use ragged-right justification but also to use some hyphenation to avoid inordinately short lines. Here is a macro for LaTeX that allows you to adjust the degree of raggedness and hyphenation. It even works when the font size is substantially changed.

```
%------ Hyphenation with ragged right
%------ by Donald Arseneau
\def\raggedright{\let\\=\@centercr
    \@rightskip\z@ plus .3\hsize
%-- reduce the above "plus" for
%-- less raggedness and more hyphenation
    \rightskip\@rightskip
    \leftskip\z@skip
    \pretolerance=1
    \hyphenpenalty=1  \exhyphenpenalty=1
    \parindent\z@}
```

To use this line formatting style, place this macro in a style file for your document (see Section 7.3), or, equivalently, place this macro in your document preamble between the `\makeatletter` and `\makeatother` commands. Then place the command `\raggedright` after the `\begin{document}` statement. If you want to restrict `\raggedright` to only a portion of your document, place that portion with the declaration `\raggedright` inside a `minipage` environment.

2.6   Headings

Sectioning commands, i.e., \part, \chapter, \section, \subsection, \subsub-
section, \paragraph, and \subparagraph, are used to produce titles for the various parts of a document. These commands generally produce a title with the
appropriate number as a prefix, make an entry in the table of contents, and also
take an optional argument for the table of contents entry if different from the section title. The general form is

\section[*table-of-contents entry*]{*heading for text*}

LaTeX automatically numbers section titles down to some specified level of sectioning below which no numbers are affixed to the title. Parts are level -1 (0 for
article style); chapters, level 0; sections, level 1; subsections, level 2; and so
on. Section numbers are generated down to a level determined by the counter
secnumdepth whose default value is 2 (3 for article style). Thus, to number only
chapters and sections (that is, down to section depth 1), put the following statement
in the document preamble.

\setcounter{secnumdepth}{1}

2.6.1   Headings without Numbers

To produce a title without any numbers, incrementing of counters, or an entry in
the table of contents, use the form

\section*{*heading for section*}

2.6.2   Breaking a Long Heading Where You Want
the Heading Broken

If you give a long section title, LaTeX will try to break it into multiple lines using
hyphenation and right justification. You can force breaks in the heading by using
\protect\newline. For example, the preceding heading was produced by

```
\subsection[Breaking a Long Heading]{Breaking a Long Heading
Where You Want \protect\newline The Heading Broken}
```

2.7   Consistent Underlining

Generally, underlining is not used in a typeset document; however, for those occasions when underlining is necessary care must be taken. For example, the input

```
\underline{Here is a test.} \underline{Here is a good test.}
```

produces <u>Here is a test.</u> Here is a good test.

This ugly result arises because the argument of the second \underline has a descender (the **g**) and the first doesn't. Hence the second underline will be lower. You can make all the underlines act as if they had descenders by inserting a \strut command. The above example can be fixed by writing

```
\underline{\strut Here is a test.}
\underline{\strut Here is a good test.}
```

to give <u>Here is a test.</u> <u>Here is a good test.</u>

Techniques for underlining and striking through large portions of the text can be done better with a macro given in Section 9.2.2.

2.8 Vertical and Horizontal Spacing

To move a block of text (for example, a list) down (or up) the page, use the \vspace{*dist*} command, where positive (or negative) *dist* is the amount of vertical movement desired, for example, .2in or -3cm. Thus to squeeze more onto a page, you could reduce the amount of vertical space between a section heading and the first paragraph by placing \vspace{-.1in} before the paragraph. To make a vertical space at the top of a page, use the \vspace*{*dist*} form of the command, since \vspace without the * is ignored at the top of a page.

Horizontal movement on a line is controlled with the \hspace{*dist*} command, where positive (negative) *dist* is the amount of right (left) shifting desired. At the beginning of a line, use \hspace*{*dist*}.

2.8.1 Variable Space

Another useful trick   for controlling horizontal spacing is provided by the "rubber length" \fill, which expands to fill all remaining space on a line. The first line of this paragraph is produced by

```
\noindent Another useful trick \hspace{\fill} for
controlling horizontal\\space is provided by the...
```

A short form of the \hspace{\fill} command is \hfill. Often, when LaTeX gives a warning of an underfilled \hbox on some page, the warning can be avoided by using an \hfill command to fill up the offending line. Similarly, \vspace{\fill}, or its equivalent \vfill, is used to expand vertical space on a page.

The \hfill command is also very useful for producing three-part headers, such as

Left Title   CENTER TITLE   **Right Title**

This was produced with

> {\bf Left Title} \hfill {\Large CENTER TITLE} \hfill {\bf Right Title}

Also commands \dotfill and \hrulefill fill the stretchable space with dots or a rule. For example,

> {\bf Left Part of Text} \dotfill {\bf Right Part of Text}
> {\bf Left Part of Text} \hrulefill {\bf Right Part of Text}

produces

Left Part of Text ....**Right Part of Text**
Left Part of Text _____**Right Part of Text**

2.9   Text in Boxes

In many instances, you will want to constrain text to a block. LaTeX has the following two commands:

> \parbox[*position*]{*width*}{*text string*}
> \begin{minipage}[*position*]{*width*} ... \end{minipage}

The \parbox command is only for simple text (no \commands), whereas the more robust minipage environment allows LaTeX commands to be included. The optional vertical placement parameter *position* is omitted if the box is to be centered vertically with the line, or use t (b) for top (bottom) alignment with the line.

Text (or a block of text in a \parbox) can be put into a ruled or unruled box with the commands

> \makebox[*width*][*position*]{*text string*}
> \framebox[*width*][*position*]{*text string*}
> \raisebox{*upshift*}[*boxheight*][*boxdepth*]{*text string*}

In the \makebox and \framebox (or \fbox for short) the *position* parameter is omitted for centering the contents in the box or specified as l (r) for left (right) justification. In the \raisebox command, the optional parameters *boxheight* and *boxdepth* are the height and depth of the box above and below the baseline of text, while *upshift* is the upward displacement of the text (positive or negative).

For example, text can or │ into a box with │ or *raised* or *lowered* with the statements
even be │ a frame
put into
a box

```
For example, \parbox[t]{.5in}{text can even be put into a box}
or \framebox{\parbox[t]{0.9in}{into a box with a frame}} or
\raisebox{.4ex}{\em raised} or \raisebox{-.6ex}{\em lowered}
with the statements
```

To adjust the separation between the frame and a box's contents, change the \fbox parameter, for example, \setlength{\fboxsep}{.3in}. The rule width can also be altered with, for example, \setlength{\fboxrule}{3pt}.

2.9.1 Right-justifying a Box

One difficulty with using a \parbox is that its horizontal placement must be obtained by trial and error. Only if the line is blank to the left of the \parbox is it possible to specify the absolute position of the right or left margin.

> This small block of text is right justified on the page with a width of 3 inches on a page with a normal text width of 6 inches. This format is useful, for example, if you want to leave a space for a small paste-in figure.

This structure was produced by

```
\hspace{\fill} \parbox{3in}{This small block of text ...
```

Sometimes you will not know how wide to make a box. Here is an example that uses the \rightline command to right justify a block of text so that the longest line is placed adjacent to the right margin

> Prof. Tom Thumb
> Dept. of Milli Engineering
> Micro State University
> NanoCity, PicoState 66502

This was produced with

```
\rightline{%
   \begin{tabular}{@{}l@{}}
      Prof.~Tom Thumb\\
      Dept.~of Milli Engineering\\
      Micro State University\\
      NanoCity, PicoState 66502
   \end{tabular}}
```

2.9.2   Paragraphs with Hanging Indents

Hanging Indent: Sometimes you may want to create a labeled paragraph like this that has a hanging indent of arbitrary length. This cannot be done with the \parbox command since you do not know *a priori* the width of the paragraph to be set after the hanging indent. Rather you must use a TeX solution and define a macro for such a paragraph.

The Method: To create paragraphs like these, place \let\hangafter\@hangfrom in your style file (or between \makeatletter and makeatother in your document's preamble). Then, to create a paragraph like the first one in this section, use

```
\hangafter{Hanging Indent: }Sometimes you may want to ...
```

2.9.3   A Macro for Indentation

An alternative to the use of \parbox to redefine the left and right margins for the text is to use the list environment to customize how the blocks of text should be placed on the page. This can be accomplished most easily by defining a new environment (such as that below for indenting text) in the preamble of your document.

```
\newenvironment{inmargins}[1]{\begin{list}{}{
    \leftmargin=#1 \rightmargin=#1 \parsep=0pt
    \partopsep=0pt}\item[]}{\end{list}}
```

This environment can be invoked whenever you wish to move both the left and the right margins in from their normal values for an entire paragraph. Simply put the desired text between \begin{inmargins}{*indent*} and end{inmargins}, where *indent* is the desired left and right margin indentations. This technique is preferable to using a \parbox since \ commands can now be embedded in the text.

This is an example paragraph that has been indented with the used of the inmargins environment. It is produced by

```
\begin{inmargins}{1.00in}
    This is an example paragraph that has been indented ...
\end{inmargins}
```

Section 9.2.6 provides a more complex macro that allows independent right and left margin indentation, as well as nesting of the indentation environments.

2.9.4   Centering Boxes

Horizontal Centering

Blocks of text (and entities such as tables and figures) are easily centered horizontally on a page with the \begin{center} ... \end{center} commands. Here is an example:

> This is a small box
> of text that is cen-
> tered.

These centering commands can be used in most environments.

```
Blocks of text (and entities such
as tables and figures) are easily
centered horizontally on a page
with the \verb|\begin{center}|
\verb|...| \verb|\end{center}|
commands.  Here is an example:
\begin{center}
  \parbox{1in}{This is a small
      box of text that is
        centered.}
\end{center}
These centering commands can be
used in most environments.
```

Vertical Centering

A box of text (or any other LaTeX entity) can also be centered vertically on a page with the following construct.

```
\newpage
\vspace*{\fill}
    .... text or item to be vertically centered ...
\vspace{\fill}
\newpage
```

2.10   Lists

In many documents, you will want to present a list of indented or itemized sentences or phrases. LaTeX provides the following three environments for making lists. These environments can be nested inside each other.

2.10.1   Itemized List

The `itemize` environment is used to make a list with each item set off by a bullet (or other symbol for an inner-nested `itemize` environment).

Here is an "itemized" list with another embedded one.

- Itemized lists are handy for listing key points
- However, don't forget:
  - The 'item' command
  - The 'end' command

```
Here is an ''itemized" list
with another embedded one.
\begin{itemize}
  \item Itemized lists are handy
        for listing key points
  \item However, don't forget:
    \begin{itemize}
      \item The 'item' command
      \item The 'end' command
    \end{itemize}
\end{itemize}
```

Changing Symbols for Itemized Lists

The symbols that begin each item in the `itemize` environment are controlled by four parameters: `\labelitemi`, `\labelitemii`, `\labelitemiii`, and `\labelitemiv`. Thus, to change the default bullet to a right arrow for the first level of itemization, put in the preamble

```
\renewcommand{\labelitemi}{$\rightarrow$} % first level
```

Similarly, for higher levels of itemization,

```
\renewcommand{\labelitemii}{$\aast$}     % second level
\renewcommand{\labelitemiii}{$Box$}      % third level
\renewcommand{\labelitemiv}{$\rhd$}      % fourth level
```

Two-column Itemized Lists

Nested list environments and boxes can be combined to produced customized lists. Here is a two-column itemized list nested within another itemized list.

- Item 1
  - Subitem 1   description of subitem 1-1
  - Subitem 2   description of subitem 1-2
- Item 2
  - Subitem 1   description of subitem 2-1 which is a long subitem extending over several lines to test the indentation
  - Subitem 2   description of subitem 2-2

This example was produced with the following input. Note especially the `\parbox` used to keep the long description of subitem 2-1 within column 2. Also this `\parbox` has to be followed by `\vspace{2\itemsep}` to produce the correct vertical spacing before the next subitem.

```
\begin{itemize}
 \item Item 1
   \begin{itemize}
   \item \makebox[1.3in][l]{Subitem 1} description of subitem 1-1
   \item \makebox[1.3in][l]{Subitem 2} description of subitem 1-2
   \end{itemize}
 \item Item 2
   \begin{itemize}
   \item \makebox[1.3in][l]{Subitem 1}
        \parbox[t]{3.0in}{description of subitem 2-1
          which is a long subitem extending over several lines
          to test the indentation} \vspace{2\itemsep}
   \item \makebox[1.3in][l]{Subitem 2} description of subitem 2-2
   \end{itemize}
\end{itemize}
```

2.10.2 Enumerated Lists

LaTeX also has an **enumerate** environment that numbers each item. The numbers are indented from the left margin.

Here is a simple example of an enumerated list:

1. Each item is sequentially assigned a number identifier
2. Don't forget the 'begin' and 'end' commands

```
Here is a simple example of
an enumerated list:
\begin{enumerate}
\item  Each item is sequentially
       assigned a number identifier
\item  Don't forget the 'begin' and
       'end' commands
\end{enumerate}
```

Changing the Enumeration Counters

Enumerate environments can be nested, and each level usually has a different style of item counter. The default counters for each level are as follows: level 1, arabic numbers; level 2, alphabetic characters; level 3, roman numerals; and level 4, uppercase alphabetic characters.

These default counters can be changed. For example, to use [i], [ii], ... for the first level enumerate environment, define \theenumi counter as

$$\def\theenumi{\roman{enumi}}$$

Then redefine the label-making command, \labelenumi, to put square brackets around the number:

$$\def\labelenumi{[\theenumi]}$$

In the same way, the style for the counters **enumii**, **enumiii**, and **enumiv** can also be modified.

2.10.3   Lists with Key Words

LaTeX also has a `description` environment that allows a title or key word to be outdented for each indented paragraph (item).

Here is a simple example of a short description list. Note the lack of indentation at the left page margin.

itemize: Bullets are used to emphasize each item of the list in this environment.

enumerate: Each item is numbered.

description: Each item has a key word (or phrase) to identify it.

```
Here is a simple example of a short
description list. Note the lack of
indentation at the left page margin.
\begin{description}
\item[itemize:] Bullets are used to
          emphasize each item of the
          list in this environment.
\item[enumerate:] Each item is
          numbered.
\item[description:] Each item has
          a key word (or phrase) to
          identify it.
\end{description}
```

2.11   Customized Lists

You can format a list in a great variety of ways by using the `list` environment. The syntax for this environment is

> \begin{list}{*default label*}{*declarations*} *list of items* \end{list}

Here *list of items* is the items to be listed, *default label* is the item label to be used if an item does not have the optional argument, as in `\item[item label]`, and *declarations* are commands that change the formatting of the list. There are many `list` formatting parameters; these are defined in Appendix B and are shown graphically in Fig. 2.1.

2.11.1   Examples of the List Environment

Here is a simple example that changes the list symbol and spacing between items.

☐ This is the first item in the new list environment.

☐ This is a second item.

And now back to the main text that follows the list.

```
... spacing between items.
\begin{list}{$\Box$}{\parsep 0in
                \itemsep .2cm}
\item This is the first item in
        the new list environment.
\item This is a second item.
\end{list}
And now back to the main text ...
```

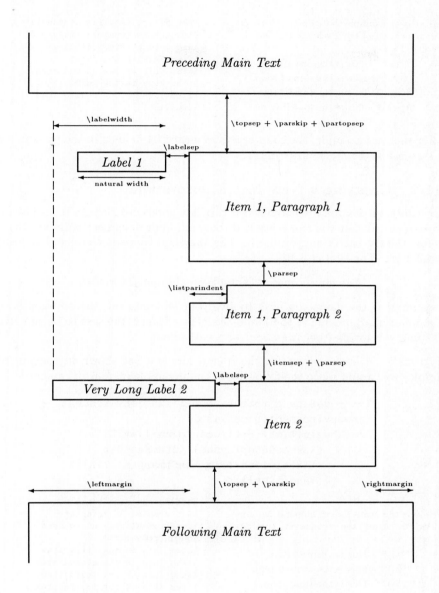

Figure 2.1: Layout of the `list` environment showing the parameters that control the positioning of the various elements.

Here is an example that shows how to use your own numbering scheme for items in a list.

```
\begin{list}{**(\roman{mynum})**}%
{\usecounter{mynum} \itemsep 0in
\labelwidth .5in \leftmargin .7in}
\item This is the first item.
\item This is the second item.
\item This is the third item.
\item This is the fourth item.
\end{list}
```

  (i) This is the first item.
  (ii) This is the second item.
  (iii) This is the third item.
  (iv) This is the fourth item.

For this last example, the counter `mynum` must first defined in the preamble with the statement `\newcounter{mynum}`.

2.11.2 Creating a New List Environment

Once you have created a customized list, it is a good idea to turn it into a special environment so that you can reuse it throughout your document without having to redefine the list each time you use it. The `\newenvironment` command is designed for this task. The syntax is

$$\text{\texttt{\textbackslash newenvironemnt}}\{name\}[args]\{begdef\}\{enddef\}$$

where *name* is the name you wish to give your environment, the optional [*args*] is the number of arguments (1 to 9), and *begdef* or *enddef* is the text to be substituted each time you invoke `\begin{name}` or `\end{name}`.

To make an environment for the roman numeral list shown in the preceding example, you would place the following in the preamble of your document.[1]

```
%---- define a roman numeral list environment
\newenvironment{romanlist}%
    {\begin{list}{**(\roman{mynum})**}%
       {\usecounter{mynum} \itemsep 0in
        \labelwidth .5in \leftmargin .7in}}%
    {\end{list}}
```

Here is the same roman numeral list created by using the `romanlist` environment.

  (i) This is the first item.
  (ii) This is the second item.
  (iii) This is the third item.
  (iv) This is the fourth item.

```
Here is the same roman numeral
list created by using the
\verb|romanlist| environment.
\begin{romanlist}
\item This is the first item.
\item This is the second item.
\item This is the third item.
\item This is the fourth item.
\end{romanlist}
```

---

[1] There cannot be spaces between the arguments of the `\newenvironment` command (or of any other LaTeX command); hence the use of `%` at some of the line ends of this macro to avoid inserting an end-of-line space.

2.11.3   Example List Environments

Reference Listing Environment

Here is an example macro to create an environment, called `reflist`, that produces an indented list with the first line of each item outdented slightly.

```
%------ environment for outdenting 1st line of each paragraph
%        ***** NOTE insert blank line after \begin{reflist}
\newenvironment{reflist}{\begin{list}{}{\listparindent -.25in
        \leftmargin .5in} \item \  \vspace{-.35in} }{\end{list}}
```

The references are then placed between `\begin{reflist}`...`\end{reflist}`, each as a separate paragraph begun by a blank line. This environment produces lists such as

> J. K. Shultis and T. R. Hill, "The Discrete Eigenvalue Problem for Azimuthally Dependent Transport Theory, *Nucl. Sci. Engg.*, **59**, 53-56 (1976).
>
> J. P. Odom and J. K. Shultis, "Anisotropic Multigroup Neutron Transport without Legendre Expansions," *Trans. Am. Nucl. Soc.*, **21**, 530 (1975).
>
> S. Lindahl and J. K. Shultis, "Fast Neutron Transmission Near Cross Section Minima," *Trans. Am. Nucl. Soc.*, **22**, 809 (1975).

This list is produced by

```
\begin{reflist}

        reference 1 ...

        reference 2 ...

        reference 3 ...
\end{reflist}
```

Note that no `\item` command is needed. In effect this environment treats all the references as a single item in which each is a separate paragraph.

Aligned List Environment

Sometimes you may wish that a "description" list have the descriptions all aligned on the left. As an example, consider

First Item: This is the description of the first item, which may extend over two or more lines, as this particular item does.

Second Item: This is the second item. It is short.

Third Item: This is a third item, which is intermediate in length between the first and second items.

This aligned description list environment `deflist` is very similar to LaTeX's `list` environment. It is defined by placing the following in the preamble (or style file):

```
\newlength{\defitemindent} \setlength{\defitemindent}{.25in}
\newcommand{\deflabel}[1]{\hspace{\defitemindent}\bf #1\hfill}
\newenvironment{deflist}[1]%
{\begin{list}{}
  {\itemsep=10pt  \parsep=5pt  \topsep=0pt  \parskip=10pt
  \settowidth{\labelwidth}{\hspace{\defitemindent}\bf #1}%
  \setlength{\leftmargin}{\labelwidth}%
  \addtolength{\leftmargin}{\labelsep}%
  \renewcommand{\makelabel}{\deflabel}}}%
{\end{list}}%
```

The parameters controlling the spacing between items and the indentation of the descriptions are easily changed. Also, the style used for the descriptors can be modified by changing the preceding \deflabel and \settowidth statements. The `deflabel` environment is used as follows:

```
\begin{deflist}{Longest Descriptor}
    \item[descriptor 1] text for first item
    \item[descriptor 2] text for second item
    ....
\end{deflist}
```

2.12   The `Verbatim` **Environment**

The `verbatim` environment uses the fixed pitch typewriter font \tt to produce an exact listing of the input. LaTeX makes no effort to interpret any of the input placed between \begin{verbatim} and \end{verbatim}. With this environment computer code listings or output containing LaTeX commands and special characters can be produced. The `verbatim` environment can handle only a few pages of input before LaTeX runs out of memory. If a very long listing is to be made, break the listing into several sequential `verbatim` environments and use \vspace{-xxin} to eliminate the break normally produced between adjacent `verbatim` outputs. In Section 8.2, a better way for producing long verbatim lists is discussed.

For verbatim text in normal lines of text, use the command `\verb`|*verbatim text*|. The delimiter | can be any character (other than *) that is not contained in *verbatim text*. Beware that such in-line verbatim text is not broken by LaTeX at the end of lines; to avoid this, several sequential `\verb`|...| should be used for lengthy verbatim text to allow LaTeX to create proper line breaks.

There are also the command variations `\begin{verbatim*}` and `\verb*` that cause a space in the verbatim input to be printed as ␣ rather than as a normal space.

Chapter 3

Formatting Pages

3.1   Page Layout

A LaTeX page has three main components: the head, the main body, and the foot. The size and positioning of these pieces are controlled by various parameters that the user can reset from their default values. The names and purposes of these page layout parameters are shown graphically in Fig. 3.1. To reset some of these parameters from their default values, you would place in the preamble of your document something similar to the following.

```
\oddsidemargin .25in    \evensidemargin .25in   \textwidth 6in
\topmargin    -.40in    \headheight .3in        \headsep  .4in
\textheight   8.4in     \footheight .2in        \footskip .7in
```

The definitions of these and other page layout parameters are defined in Appendix B. Of special note here is the abbreviated TeX way in which the page layout parameters are specified. The more conventional way would be to use LaTeX's \setlength command; for example,

```
\setlength{\oddsidemargin}{.25in}
\setlength{\evensidemargin}{.25in}
\setlength{\textwidth}{6in}
```

LaTeX also allows a two-column page layout; however, a discussion of this page format style is deferred until Section 3.7.

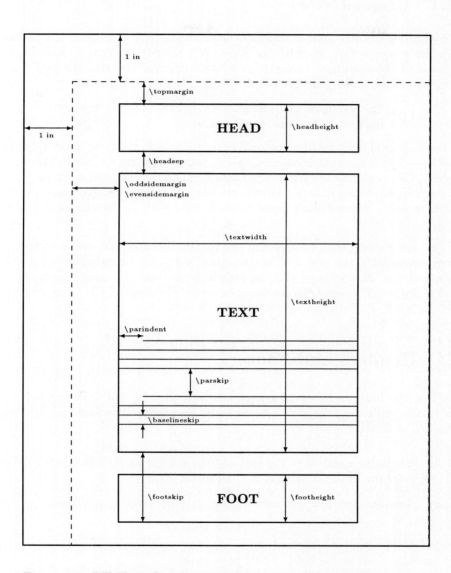

Figure 3.1: LATEX single-column page layout and the parameters used to define the dimensions of the various page components. Not shown is the location of marginal notes (see Section 3.1.1).

3.1.1 Marginal Notes

Although infrequently used in technical documents, there is a fourth page component, the marginal note. Such a note is placed in the page margin with its first line adjacent to the command \marginpar whose argument contains the text for the note. The example here was produced with

A short
margin
note

```
... The example here\marginpar{\flushleft\em A short
      margin note} was produced with
```

For one-sided printing, the marginal note is placed in the right margin, for two-sided printing in the outside margin, and in two-column documents in the nearest margin. The command \reversemarginpar reverses the left-right ordering so that, for example, on even-numbered one-column pages, margin notes appear on the right (inside margin). \normalmarginpar restores the default positioning of the margin notes.

The parameters that control the spacing of the marginal notes include (1) \marginparwidth, the width of the marginal note, (2) \marginparsep, the distance between the text body and the margin notes, and (3) \marginparpush, the vertical distance between adjacent marginal notes. See Appendix B for more details.

3.2 Headers and Footers

In LaTeX the head and foot of a page are controlled by the \pagestyle{....} declaration, with the page style's name as its argument. The four standard page styles are as follows:

plain The page number is in the foot and the head is empty. This is the default style for the article and report document styles.

empty The head and foot are both empty. A page number is assigned but not printed.

headings The page number and other information, determined by the document style, are put in the head. The foot is empty.

myheadings This is similar to the headings style except that the user must specify the "other information" that goes in the head by using the \markright and \markboth commands. The foot is empty. To place "Left Page" or "Right Page" in the head of even-numbered (left) pages or of odd-numbered (right) pages, respectively, place the following in your preamble:

```
\documentstyle{myheadings}
\markboth{Left Page}{Right Page}
```
The \markboth command can also be used anywhere in your document to change the head text. For one-sided documents, the \markright is used.

3.2.1   Head and Foot for the First Page

The styles described so far for a page's head and foot apply to all pages of a document except the first page of a chapter. The \chapter command causes a special default format to be used on the first page. This default format can be overridden by including the command \thispagestyle{*style*} somewhere in the text for the first page after the \chapter command. Here *style* is the name of the head and foot style desired. For example, on the first page of a chapter (right after the \chapter command), there might be the statement \thispagestyle{myheadings}.

Even though you specify \pagestyle{empty} to force an empty head and foot, a bug in LaTeX will still place a centered page number in the foot of the first page of a chapter. To create an empty first page, place \thispagestyle{empty} somewhere in the input for the first page.

3.2.2   A Head and Foot Macro

Here is a macro to create a head and foot that are both separated from the text by horizontal rules. This macro produces page layouts similar to those below.

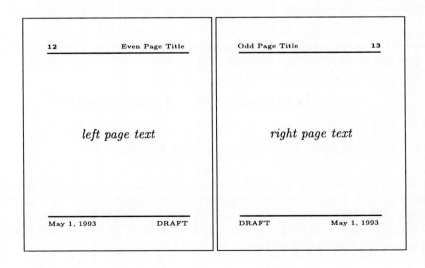

To produce such heads and feet for a two-sided document, place the following macro in the preamble of your document.

```
\makeatletter
\def\@evenhead{
        \vbox{\hbox to\hsize{\bf \thepage \hfill \sl \leftmark}
        \vspace{2pt} \hbox to\hsize{\hrulefill}}}
\def\@oddhead{
        \vbox{\hbox to\hsize{\sl \rightmark \hfill \bf \thepage}
        \vspace{2pt} \hbox to\hsize{\hrulefill}}}
\def\@evenfoot{\vbox{ \hbox to\hsize{\hrulefill}
        \vspace{-40pt} \hbox to\hsize{\today \hfill \sl \footmsg}}}
\def\@oddfoot{\vbox{ \hbox to\hsize{\hrulefill}
        \vspace{-40pt} \hbox to\hsize{\sl \footmsg \hfill \rm \today}}}
\makeatother
```

Note that these definitions use LaTeX variables `\today` and `\thepage` to supply the date and page number. User-supplied variables `\leftmark`, `\rightmark`, and `\footmsg` are used to place labels in the head and foot definitions. These variables are defined in the document preamble (or redefined anywhere in the document when the head or foot label is to be changed) as

```
\def\leftmark{Even Page Title}
\def\rightmark{Odd Page Title}
\def\footmsg{DRAFT}
```

This macro is for a two-sided 12-point document with a `\footskip` of 0.7 inch. For a different value of `\footskip` and font size, the `\vspace{-40pt}` shift for the foot will have to be changed. In practice, it takes some fiddling with the foot spacing parameters and the foot style definition to get the desired foot placement.

Instead of placing the preceding macro in the preamble, you could place it, *without* the `\makeatletter` and `\makeatother` statements, in a separate style file (say, NEWHDFT.STY). Then any document can use this style file by specifying it as a style option in the `\documentstyle` command; that is,

```
\documentstyle[newhdft,twoside,12pt]{report}
```

3.2.3   More Elaborate Headers and Footers

A far easier way to design a pages's foot and head than that just described is to use the style file known as FANCYHEADS.STY (also known by its shortened name FANCYHDS.STY). This style file allows very elaborate multiline heads and feet to be created with different styles for the first and subsequent pages. Detailed notes on how to use FANCYHDS.STY are given in Section 8.7.

3.3   Blank Pages

Sometimes you will want to leave one or more pages blank for paste-in figures or other data produced outside LaTeX. Two ways are suggested here.

Method 1:

At the place in the document where you want the blank pages to begin, insert the command `\clearpage` to begin a new page. Then for every blank page desired add the line `~\clearpage`. The `~` is needed to trick LaTeX into thinking that there is something on the blank page (here a single interword space) and hence that a new page should be started. This method has the advantage (or disadvantage depending on your point of view) of physically producing blank pages (complete with heads and feet, if any) when the document is printed. If many blank pages are needed, this can be very wasteful of paper. Method 2 avoids this problem.

Method 2:

At the place in the text where you want the blank pages to begin, issue the `\clearpage` command. Then reset the page number counter to the number of the page following the last blank page, nn, with the command `\setcounter{page}{`nn`}`. Better yet, just increment the page counter with `\addtocounter{page}{`m`}`, where m is the number of blank pages to be inserted into the document. When the document is printed, the blanks pages will thus be skipped, and the printed pages will be correctly numbered.

3.4   Widows and Orphans

Although LaTeX is very clever when composing a page, it occasionally produces "widows" (the last line of a paragraph placed alone at the top of a page) and "orphans" (the first line of a paragraph at the bottom of a page). I have not found the `\pagebreak`, `\nopagebreak` and `\samepage{...}` commands to be very effective at preventing a paragraph from losing its first or last line.

An inelegant way to avoid a single line at the bottom of the page (an orphan) is to place a `\clearpage` command just before the orphaned paragraph. To avoid placing the last line of a paragraph at the top of a page (a widow), the use of `\vspace{-.1in}` in one or more spots on the previous page (for example, before and/or after section titles) will tighten the page and leave room for the last line of the paragraph.

A more elegant solution (at the cost of LaTeX complaining about over- and under-filled pages) is to increase the penalty for orphans and widows by placing the following in the preamble.

`\clubpenalty=10000`   `\widowpenalty=10000`

3.5 Counters

LaTeX has many counters and even allows users to define their own counters. Some of the frequently used LaTeX counters are `page, equation, footnote, chapter, section, subsection, table,` and `figure`. The values of these counters can be reset or incremented with

$$\text{\textbackslash setcounter}\{counter\}\{nn\}$$
$$\text{\textbackslash addtocounter}\{counter\}\{nn\}$$

NOTE: All counters, *except* `page`, are incremented before being used by LaTeX; thus set the counter to one less than the value you want used. For the page counter, set it to the value to be used next.

The current value of any counter can be printed with the \the*counter* command. The font style used for printing the counter can be set with

\arabic{*counter*}	use arabic numbers
\roman{*counter*}	use lowercase roman numerals
\Roman{*counter*}	use uppercase roman numerals
\alph{*counter*}	use a lowercase letter
\Alph{*counter*}	use an uppercase letter

To create a new counter called `mycounter`, put `\newcounter{mycounter}` in the preamble of your document. The value of this counter can then be set to the value 84, for example, with the command `\setcounter{mycounter}{84}`. Then the sequence

```
{\em mycounter} has the value \themycounter\ or \Roman{mycounter}.
```

would produce *mycounter* has the value 84 or LXXXIV.

3.6 Floats

A float is a block of material (usually a figure or table) that is preserved as a single unbreakable unit whose placement in the document is determined by LaTeX and not by where it is placed in the input file. LaTeX tries to put a float near to the place where it is first referenced in the text, typically right after the paragraph containing the reference to the float or on the next page.

The two environments used to create floating units, the `table` and `figure` environments, behave very similarly. The main difference is that `table` writes captions as "Table 3.1:..." and makes entries in the `.lot` file, whereas `figure` uses "Figure 3.1:..." and makes entries in the `.lof` file. A float is created by

\begin{table}[*placement*]
    table input, caption, label
\end{table}
	\begin{figure}[*placement*]
	    caption, label, figure input
	\end{figure}

The *placement* parameter can be h (here), t (top), b (bottom), p (page), or any combination of these letter, for example, [htbp]. The placement h specifies that the float is to be printed where it appears in the input; that is, it will *not* float unless there is insufficient space on the page, in which case its printing is delayed (sweeping all subsequent floats with it) until a \clearpage is encountered. The placement notation t (or b) indicates that the float is to be put at the top (or bottom) of the present or on a following text page. Finally, p says that the float is to appear on a page of floats (a page without any text). If possible, it is always best to specify [htbp] to avoid a piling up of floating objects, which will eventually cause LaTeX to run out of memory.

3.6.1 Positioning Floats

The positioning of floats is controlled by many positioning parameters (see Appendix B) and by several restrictive rules. Some important parameters and restrictions are shown below for the three float placement types [h], [b], and [p]. (The fourth placement type [t] is similar to [b] with \bottomfraction replaced by \topfraction.) Examples of how to change the values of these and other float control parameters are given in Section 3.6.4.

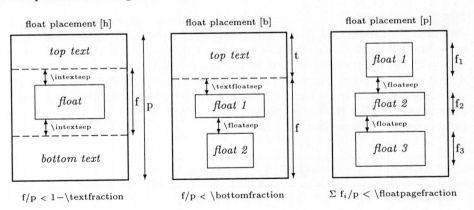

3.6.2 Keeping a Group of Tables or Figures Together

Within the scope of a table or figure environment, you can define multiple tables and figures, each with an optional caption and label, in order to keep the group of tables and figures together as a single floating block. Similarly, two adjacent minipages can be used to place two tables or figures side by side and to keep the pair as a single floating object (see Section 5.4.3).

3.6.3   Piling up of Floats

There can be problems with outputting many floating figures and tables in LaTeX, notably when a whole collection of floats drifts to the end of a chapter or document. This occurs when a float cannot be printed where specified (usually because of an [h] placement). All subsequent floats are then held up until the first float is finally printed at the end of the chapter or document. One way to avoid this piling up of floats is to place a \clearpage command in the input, thereby forcing the printing of all floats regardless of their placement specification.

Similarly, a document containing a large number of floats, all specifying a placement of [t] say, will have the floats spread over many pages with some ending up far from their references in the text. Always use [htbp], if possible, to allow LaTeX to print the floats as close to their initial reference as possible. Remember, the float placement specification is really a *restriction* on where floats may appear.

3.6.4   Putting Many Floats on a Page

LaTeX does not like to have many floats on a page or only a little text on a page containing both text and floats. For a document with many small floats, this can cause the floats to become far too spread out in the document. By adjusting in the preamble the parameters that LaTeX uses to control the output of floats (see Appendix B), you can put many more floats on a single page. The following values will cause all floats to be output when defined or, if there is insufficient space on the current page, at the top of the next page. Sometimes this produces ugly page breaks, but this can be fixed manually.

Parameter	Old	New	Function
topnumber	2	5	max. floats allowed at top
\topfraction	.7	.9	max. fraction of floats vs. text at top
bottomnumber	1	5	max. floats allowed at bottom
\bottomfraction	.3	.9	max. fraction of floats vs. text at bottom
totalnumber	3	10	max. floats per page
\textfraction	.2	.05	min. fraction of page that must be text
\floatpagefraction	.5	.05	min. fraction of page used for floats

To set these float parameters, put in the preamble commands such as

```
\setcounter{topnumber}{5}
\renewcommand{\topfraction}{.9}
```

The results are surprisingly good. However, you do get a number of bad page breaks when there are large (over 3 inches in height) figures or tables, or several small floats defined on one page. There are probably a number of other choices of parameter values that will work; these were rather empirically chosen. Finally, `\floatpagefraction` should always be greater that both `\topfraction` and `bottomfraction` to prevent a float, which is between these sizes (and hence not allowed on a mixed page), causing a pile up of subsequent floats.

3.7   Two-column Format

LaTeX can also typeset pages in a two-column format. To produce a two-column document, specify the `twocolumn` option in the `\documentstyle` command:

```
\documentstyle[12pt,twocolumn]{report}.
```

In a single-column document, you can switch to double-column format by issuing the `\twocolumn` command and return to one-column format with `\onecolumn`. Note that with these options you cannot mix one- and two-column formats on the same page. A new page is begun each time you change the column format.

If you wish to alternate between one- and two-column format on the same page or to use more than two columns, the `MULTICOL.STY` style file discussed in Section 8.9 is recommended.

3.7.1   Page Layout

The layout of a two-column page and the parameters that control the layout are shown in Fig. 3.2.

3.7.2   Spanning Both Columns

In the two-column style, text and floats are normally placed within the margins of a single column. However, sometimes you might want the text to span both columns, for example, a title block at the top of the first page. Simply use the `\twocolumn[ ... ]` environment to have the contents between the square brackets span both columns. For example, a simple title block can be produced with

```
\twocolumn[\centering {\bf A TITLE CENTERED OVER BOTH COLUMNS}]
```

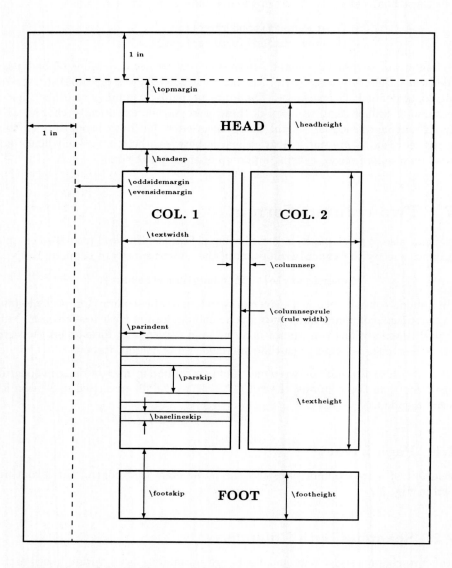

Figure 3.2: LaTeX two-column page layout and the parameters used to define the dimensions of the various page components. Not shown is the marginal notes component.

3.7.3   Floats in Two-column Format

In a two-column format, the `table` and `figure` environments normally occupy one column. However, a figure or table may occupy both columns (extend across the entire page) by using the `figure*` or `table*` environments. For floats using both columns, the placement arguments [h] and [b] are not allowed.

3.7.4   Clearing Pages and Columns

In two-column format, the `\newpage` and `\pagebreak` commands start a new column rather than a new page. However, the `\clearpage` and `\cleardoublepage` commands cause a new page to begin.

3.7.5   Marginal Notes

Marginal notes in two-column format are placed in the margin adjacent to the column in which the `\marginpar` command is issued. The parameters for controlling the size and placement of marginal notes are given in Appendix B.

Chapter 4

Math and Equations

4.1 Displaying Math Expressions

Two basic types of formula (or math) environments are available in LaTeX: (1) a text mode in which math expressions are placed in a line of text, and (2) a display environment in which the math expression is place on a separate line.

text mode: To place a math expression in a line of text, simply enclose the math expression with $...$ or, equivalently, \(...\). In this mode, some symbols such as $\int_a^b$ and $\sum_{i=1}^n$ are written more compactly compared to their treatment in the "displaymath" mode.

displaymath (without equation numbering): To center a math expression or formula on a separate line, embed the math expression between the environment delimiters \begin{displaymath} ... \end{displaymath}. Shorthand equivalents are \[...\] or $$...$$.

displaymath (with equation numbering): To place automatically an equation number to the right of a math expression that is centered on a separate line, use the \begin{equation} ... \end{equation} environment. There is no built-in shorthand equivalent (although a shorthand version can be defined in the preamble; see Section 7.2).

4.2 Composing Math Expressions

In LaTeX, a large variety of mathematical expressions can be created; however, you often have to resort to fairly complex programming for "difficult" expressions. These difficult expressions are handled much more easily with the macros of $\mathcal{AMS}$-LaTeX. However, in these notes we stick to pure LaTeX (mixed occasionally with TeX). Here are some examples.

Fractions

$$\frac{x+y^2}{k+1} \qquad y^{\frac{2}{k+1}} \qquad y^{2/(k+1)}$$

```
\frac{x+y^2}{k+1}\qquad
y^{\frac 2{k+1}}\qquad y^{2/(k+1)}
```

$$\frac{\frac{a}{b}}{2} \qquad \frac{a}{\frac{b}{2}} \qquad \frac{a/b}{2}$$

```
\frac{\frac ab}2 \qquad
\frac a{\frac b2}\qquad\frac{a/b}2
```

$$a_0+\frac{1}{a_1+\frac{1}{a_2+\frac{1}{a_3+\frac{1}{a_4}}}}$$

```
a_0+\frac{1}{a_1+\frac{1}
{a_2+\frac{1}{a_3+\frac{1}{a_4}}}}
```

$$a_0+\frac{1}{a_1+\frac{1}{a_2+\frac{1}{a_3+\frac{1}{a_4}}}}$$

```
a_0+\frac{1}{a_1+\frac{\textstyle 1}
{\textstyle a_2+\frac{\textstyle 1}
{\textstyle a_3+\frac{\textstyle 1}
{\textstyle a_4}}}}
```

$$a_0+\frac{1}{a_1+\frac{1}{a_2+\frac{1}{a_3+\frac{1}{a_4}}}}$$

```
a_0+\frac{1\hfill}{a_1+\frac{
\textstyle 1\hfill}{\textstyle a_2+
\frac{\textstyle 1\hfill}{\textstyle
a_3+\frac{\textstyle 1\hfill}
{\textstyle a_4}}}}
```

Binomials

$$\frac{\binom{n+1}{k/2}}{5!}$$

```
\frac{{n+1 \choose k/2}}{5!}
```

Math Accents

$$\dot{a}\dot{A}\tilde{D}\widetilde{D}\hat{H}\widehat{H}\ \widehat{1-x}\ \vec{u}\ \vec{\imath}\ \vec{\jmath}$$

```
\dot{a} \dot{A} \tilde{D} \widetilde{D}
\hat{H} \widehat{H} \; \widehat{1-x} \;
\vec{u} \; \vec{\imath} \; \vec{\jmath}
```

Subscripts and Superscripts

$$a^{b^{c+1}} \quad 2^{(2^x)} \quad 2^{2^{2^{2^{2^x}}}} \qquad x_{y_2} \quad x_{y^2}$$

```
a^{b^{c+1}} \quad 2^{(2^x)} \quad
2^{2^{2^{2^{2^x}}}}\quad x_{y_2}
\quad x_{y^2}
```

$$A_b^a \quad \Gamma_{y_b^a}^{z_c^d} \quad {}^{\nu_c^d}_{\mu_a^b}M \quad f_+ \quad 5 \times 10^{-13}$$

```
A_b^a \quad \Gamma _{y_b^a}^{z_c^d}
\quad {}^{\nu_c^d}_{\mu_a^b}\!M
\quad f_{+} \quad 5 \times 10^{-13}
```

$$^{235}_{92}\mathrm{U} \qquad \vec{F}_K{}_i^j$$

```
{}^{235}_{\phantom{2}92}\mbox{U} \qquad
\vec{F}_{\!\scriptscriptstyle K}{}_i^j
```

Growing Symbols

$$\underline{\underline{4+x}} \quad x^{\underline{n}+m} \quad \overline{\overline{x^3}+x^{x^3}}$$

```
\underline{\underline{4+x}} \quad
x^{\underline{n}+m} \quad
\overline{\overline{x^3}+x^{x^3}}
```

$$\left[\left(x+\frac b{2a} \right)^2 +\left(\frac ca - \frac{b^2}{4a} \right) \right]$$

```
\left[ \left( x+\frac b{2a}
\right)^2 +\left( \frac ca -
\frac{b^2}{4a} \right) \right]
```

$$\left(\sqrt{\frac{A^C}{B_y}} +\sum_{i=1}^N a_i \right)$$

```
\left( \sqrt{\frac{A^C}{B_y}}
+\sum_{i=1}^Na_i\right)
```

$$\frac{a+1}b \left/ \frac{c+1}d \right.$$

```
\frac{a+1}b \left/ \frac{c+1}d
\right.
```

$$\left(\sqrt{\left(\sqrt{\left(\sqrt{\left(\sqrt{(1+x^2)} \right)} \right)} \right)} \right)$$

```
\left( \sqrt{\left( \sqrt{\left(
\sqrt{\left( \sqrt{(1+x^2)}
\right) }\right) }\right) }\right)
```

$$\underbrace{\overbrace{a,\ldots,a}^{k\ a\text{'s}},\overbrace{b,\ldots,b}^{m\ b\text{'s}}}_{n+1\ \text{elements}}$$

```
\underbrace{\overbrace{
\rule{0in}{1.6ex}a,\ldots,a}
^{k\ a\mbox{\scriptsize 's}},
\overbrace{b,\ldots,b}^{m\ b
\mbox{\scriptsize 's}}}
_{n+1\ \mbox{\scriptsize elements}}}
```

Matrices

$$A = \left(\begin{array}{cccc} a_{11} & a_{12} & \ldots & a_{1n} \\ a_{21} & a_{22} & \ldots & a_{2n} \\ \vdots & \vdots & \ddots & \vdots \\ a_{m1} & a_{m2} & \ldots & a_{mn} \end{array} \right)$$

```
A=\left( \begin{array}{cccc}
a_{11} & a_{12} & \ldots & a_{1n} \\
a_{21} & a_{22} & \ldots & a_{2n} \\
\vdots & \vdots & \ddots & \vdots \\
a_{m1} & a_{m2} & \ldots & a_{mn}
\end{array} \right)
```

$$\mathbf{S}^{-1}\mathbf{TS}=\mathbf{diag}(\omega_1,\ldots,\omega_n) = \mathbf{\Lambda}$$

```
{\bf S}^{-1}{\bf TS}={\bf diag}
(\omega_1,\ldots ,\omega_n) =
{\bf \Lambda}
```

$$\det \left| \begin{array}{lllll} c_0 & c_1 & \ldots & c_n \\ c_1 & c_2 & \ldots & c_{n+1} \\ \vdots & \vdots & & \vdots \\ c_n & c_{n+1} & \ldots & c_{2n} \end{array} \right| > 0$$

```
\det \left| \begin{array}{lllll}
c_0 & c_1 & \ldots & c_n \\
c_1 & c_2 & \ldots & c_{n+1} \\
\vdots & \vdots & & \vdots \\
c_n & c_{n+1} & \ldots & c_{2n}
\end{array} \right| >0
```

Operators

$$\equiv \quad \simeq \quad \le \quad \neq \quad \not\simeq \quad \not\le$$

```
\equiv \quad \simeq \quad
\le \quad \not\equiv \quad
\not\simeq \quad \not\le
```

$$\sum x_n \quad \sum x_n \quad \sum_{n=1}^{m} \quad \sum\nolimits_{n=1}^{m}$$

```
\mbox{$\sum x_n$} \quad \sum x_n
\quad \sum_{n=1}^m \quad
\sum\nolimits_{n=1}^m
```

$$\oint \quad \int_{\infty}^{\infty} \quad \int_{\infty}^{\infty} \quad \iint_{\Omega_s} d\Omega \; f(\Omega)$$

```
\quad \oint \quad
\mbox{$\int_{\infty}^{\infty}$}
\quad \int_{\infty}^{\infty} \quad
\int\!\!\! \int_{\bf \Omega_s}
\!\!\!d\Omega \; f({\bf \Omega})
```

$$\sum_{\substack{0\le i\le m\\0<j<n}} P(i,j) \quad \prod_{i=1}^{p}\prod_{j=1}^{q}\prod_{k=1}^{r} a_{ij}\, b_{jk}\, c_{ki}$$

```
\sum_{\stackrel{\scriptstyle 0\leq
i\leq m}{0<j<n}}\!\!\! P(i,j) \quad
\prod_{i=1}^p\prod_{j=1}^q\prod_{k=1}^r
a_{ij}\,b_{jk}\,c_{ki}
```

Text in Formulas

$$WLM = \int_{\text{month}} dt \; WL(t)$$

```
\mbox{\em WLM}=\int_{\mbox{%
\tiny month}} \! \! \! \! \!
\!\!\!\!\!\!\! dt\; \mbox{\em WL}(t)
```

$$g(x) = f(x + \text{constant})$$

```
g(x)=f(x+\mbox{constant})
```

$$\sum_{n\text{ odd}} f(x_n), \quad \text{only if } x_n < 0$$

```
\sum_{n\mbox{\scriptsize \ odd}}
f(x_n), \quad
\mbox{only if $x_n < 0$}
```

Miscellaneous

$$\iint z\, dx\, dy \quad \textbf{not} \quad \int \int z dx dy$$

```
\int\!\!\!\int z\,dx\,dy \quad
\mbox{\bf not} \quad
\int\int z dx dy
```

$$A \stackrel{\lambda_a}{\longrightarrow} B$$

```
A \stackrel{\lambda_a}
{\longrightarrow} B
```

$$^{239}\text{Pu atoms h}^{-1}$$

```
{}^{239}\mbox{Pu atoms h$^{-1}$}
```

$$\lim_{h \rightarrow \infty} \left[\; \overline{\widehat{K}(h) + \hat{K}(h)} \; \right]$$

```
\lim_{h \rightarrow \infty} \left[
\: \overline{\widehat{K}(h)
+ \hat{K}(h)} \:\right]
```

4.3   Math Spacing Commands

For many math expressions, it is important to perform some small horizontal spacing adjustments to move parts together or apart. Here are the math-mode spacing commands ($\sqcup$ indicates a space).

Space Type	Command	Example	Produced by
no space		‖	`$||$` or `$|⎵⎵⎵|$`
thin space[a]	`\,`	‖	`$|\,|$`
medium space	`\:`	‖	`$|\:|$`
thick space	`\;`	‖	`$|\;|$`
full space[a]	`\⎵`	‖	`$|\⎵|$`
quad space (1 em)[a]	`\quad`	| |	`$|\quad|$`
qquad space (2 em)[a]	`\qquad`	| |	`$|\qquad|$`
negative space	`\!`	‖	`$|\!|$`

[a] May also be used in text mode.

4.4   Types of Equations

Three basic types of equations are frequently encountered when using LaTeX: (1) simple equation, (2) multi-line or multi-conditional equations, and (3) an array of equations.

4.4.1   Simple Equations

A simple equation, such as $y(x) = 3 + x^2$ or Eq. (4.1),

$$f(x) + g(x) = \sqrt{1 + x^2} \tag{4.1}$$

is produced by

```
A simple equation, such as $y(x) = 3+x^2$
or Eq.~(\ref{simpleeq}),
\begin{equation}
        f(x) + g(x) = \sqrt{1 + x^2}
        \label{simpleeq}
\end{equation}
```

Note the use of the optional `\label` in the single-line equation definition so that this label can be referenced later in the text with `\ref{simpleeq}`.

4.4.2 Multiconditional Equations

Often an equation will have multiple lines on one side of the $=$ sign that depend on various conditions. For example,

$$f(x) = \left\{ \begin{array}{ll} z - y & \text{if } y > 0 \\ z + y & \text{otherwise} \end{array} \right. \tag{4.2}$$

is produced by

```
\begin{equation}
    f(x) = \left\{  \begin{array}{ll}
                    z-y & \mbox{if $y>0$} \\
                    z+y & \mbox{otherwise}
                    \end{array}
          \right.
    \label{eqtype2}
\end{equation}
```

Note the use of `\mbox{...}` to place roman fonts in the equation.

4.4.3 Multiline and Multiple Equations

Sometimes you will want to break a long equation into several lines or to have several equations in one block. For this, LaTeX provides the **eqnarray** environment.

$$f(x) = \sqrt{1 - x^2} \tag{4.3}$$
$$g(x) = a + b + c + d + e + f$$
$$+ g + h + i + j \tag{4.4}$$

is produced by

```
\begin{eqnarray}
    f(x) & = & \sqrt{1 - x^2}  \label{eqmulti1} \\
    g(x) & = & a + b + c + d + e + f \nonumber \\
         &   & +\ g + h + i + j  \label{eqmulti2}
\end{eqnarray}
```

Notice that when an equation is broken between lines with \\ the \nonumber command is used to prevent an equation number being automatically printed to the right of the broken line.

There is also an `eqnarray*` environment that is exactly like the `eqnarray` environment except that equation numbers are not automatically placed at the end of each equation line. To force an equation number in this environment, insert `\yesnumber` after the line and before the line break `\\`.

4.5   Equal Spacing in Equations and Eqnarrays

The spacing around the equal sign in an `eqnarray` environment is larger than that in an `equation` environment, as can be seen by comparing Eqs. (4.1) and (4.3). The spacing can be made the same for both environments by defining in the preamble the following new environment:

```
\newenvironment{Eqnarray}%
      {\arraycolsep 0.14em\begin{eqnarray}}{\end{eqnarray}}
```

Then with the use of `\begin{Eqnarray}`...`\end{Eqnarray}`, Eqs. (4.3) and (4.4) are typeset as

$$f(x) = \sqrt{1 - x^2} \qquad (4.5)$$
$$g(x) = a + b + c + d + e + f$$
$$+ \, g + h + i + j \qquad (4.6)$$

4.6   Text in Eqnarray

In the `eqnarray` environment, we often want to insert text between equations without leaving the environment and the alignment on the = sign. For example,

$$a = b + c \qquad (4.7)$$
$$d = f + g \qquad (4.8)$$

and finally
$$h = d + e + f \qquad (4.9)$$

uses `\noalign` to insert the words "and finally" between the second and third equation.

In the `{\tt eqnarray}` environment, we often want to insert text between equations without leaving the environment and the alignment on the = sign. For example,
```
    \begin{eqnarray}
    a & = & b + c \\
    d & = & f + g \\
    \noalign{\hbox{and finally}}
    h & = & d + e  + f
    \end{eqnarray}
```
uses `\verb|\noalign|` to insert the words ``and finally" between the second and third equation.

4.7   Vertical Spacing With Struts

A strut, such as \rule{0in}{.25in}, is a box of some specified height but of zero width so that nothing is printed. However, the height of a strut forces extra space above the line containing the strut. A strut can thus be used to increase spacing between lines of a multiline equation as shown in the second example below. Note the use of \s, which has been defined as a shorthand notation for a strut by the \def\s{\rule{0in}{.30in}} statement. This is a useful definition to place in the document preamble if you use a lot of struts.

$$A = \int \frac{f(x)}{g(x)} dx$$
$$+ \int \frac{h(x)}{g(x)} dx$$

```
\begin{eqnarray*}
A &=& \int \frac{f(x)}{g(x)} dx \\
  & & \quad +\int\frac{h(x)}{g(x)} dx
\end{eqnarray*}
```

$$A = \int \frac{f(x)}{g(x)} dx$$
$$+ \int \frac{h(x)}{g(x)} dx$$

```
\def\s{\rule{0in}{.30in}}
\begin{eqnarray*}
A &=& \int \frac{f(x)}{g(x)} dx \\
  & & \s \quad +
      \int\frac{h(x)}{g(x)} dx
\end{eqnarray*}
```

The strut is also useful for tricking LaTeX into thinking that the line is taller than it really is. In this way, variable delimiters (for example, \left[or \right\}) on different lines of a multiline equation can be made the same size. Consider the following examples. In the second example, a strut has been placed in the second line to force the closing square bracket to have the same size as the square bracket on the first line.

$$g(x,y) = \left[\frac{f(x,y)}{\sqrt{x-y}}\right.$$
$$\times B(x,y)e^{-\mu x}\right]$$

```
\begin{eqnarray*}
g(x,y) &=& \left[ \frac{f(x,y)}
           {\sqrt{x-y}} \right.\\
  & & \qquad \times \left.
      B(x,y) e^{-\mu x} \right]
\end{eqnarray*}
```

$$g(x,y) = \left[\frac{f(x,y)}{\sqrt{x-y}}\right.$$
$$\times B(x,y)e^{-\mu x}\right]$$

```
\begin{eqnarray*}
g(x,y) &=& \left[ \frac{f(x,y)}
           {\sqrt{x-y}} \right.\\
  & & \qquad \times \left.
      \rule{0in}{3.0ex}
      B(x,y) e^{-\mu x} \right]
\end{eqnarray*}
```

4.8   Math-mode Font Sizes

Four font sizes and styles are available in math mode: \textstyle, \displaystyle, \scriptstyle, and \scriptscriptstyle.

\displaystyle is used for *displayed equations* (equations on their own lines), whereas \textstyle is used for mathematical expressions in a line of text. These fonts are almost the same except that the large operators are different: for example, in \textstyle we get $\sum_{i=1}^{N}$ and $\int_a^b$ and in \displaystyle we get $\displaystyle\sum_{i=1}^{N}$ and $\displaystyle\int_a^b$.

The math style \scriptstyle is used for first-level superscripts and subscripts; \scriptscriptstyle is normally used for higher-level superscripts and subscripts.

4.8.1   Nested Fraction Constructions

The \frac command produces small fonts when they are nested, as in the first example below. Fonts can be returned to normal size with the \displaystyle command, as in the second example. However, the third construction is the preferred way to typeset this type of expression.

$$\frac{\frac{u}{v}}{1+\frac{x}{y}}$$

```
\frac{\frac{u}{v}}
     {1+\frac{x}{y}}
```

$$\displaystyle\frac{\displaystyle\frac{u}{v}}{1+\frac{x}{y}}$$

```
\displaystyle\frac{\displaystyle
   \frac{u}{v}}{\displaystyle
   1+\frac{x}{y}}
```

$$\frac{u/v}{1+x/y}$$

```
\frac{u/v}{1+x/y}
```

4.8.2   Displaystyle in Eqnarrays and Arrays

LaTeX has a nasty habit of using small fonts in an `array` or `eqnarray` environment (see the first example that follows). The second example shows a way to avoid this problem. Notice also in the second example that the strut (`\rule{0in}{5ex}`) is used to increase the spacing between the two lines of the array.

$$\left[\begin{array}{c} \frac{\partial f}{\partial s} \\ \frac{\partial f}{\partial t} \end{array} \right] = 0$$

```
\[            %----- 1st example
\left[
\begin{array}{c}
    \frac{\partial f}{\partial s} \\
    \frac{\partial f}{\partial t}
\end{array}
\right] = 0
\]
```

$$\left[\begin{array}{c} \dfrac{\partial f}{\partial s} \\[5ex] \dfrac{\partial f}{\partial t} \end{array} \right] = 0$$

```
\[            %----- 2nd example
{ \everymath{\displaystyle}
  \left[
  \begin{array}{c}
      \frac{\partial f}{\partial s} \\
      \rule{0in}{5ex}
      \frac{\partial f}{\partial t}
  \end{array}
  \right] = 0 }
\]
```

4.9 Manual Equation Numbering

The easiest way to gain control of equation numbers in LaTeX is not to use them! In some situations the normal LaTeX convention of *chapter.eqno* is not flexible enough and neither are most of the "subeqn" styles (see Section 8.4). But the TeX command \eqno() also works in LaTeX, so that you can write

```
$$ pV = nRT .   \eqno(\mbox{\em ideal gas law: } 12345a)$$
```

to produce

$$pV = nRT. \qquad\qquad (ideal\ gas\ law:\ 12345a)$$

4.10 Equations With Left and Right Tags

As a special effect, you may occasionally want a displayed equation to have a tag both on the left and on the right of the equation line, as in the two following examples.

$$\Longrightarrow \qquad g(x) = \int_a^b dx\, \frac{f(x)}{\sqrt{1-x^2}} \qquad a\ difficult\ integral$$

$$\Longrightarrow \qquad g(x) = \int_a^b dx\, \frac{f(x)}{\sqrt{1-x^2}} \qquad a\ difficult\ integral$$

The first example, with the equation centered on the line, is produced by

```
\[ \Longrightarrow \setbox0=\hbox{$\Longrightarrow$}\kern-\wd0
   \hspace{.5\columnwidth minus .5\columnwidth}
      g(x)=\int_a^b dx\, \frac{f(x)}{\sqrt{1-x^2}}
   \hspace{.5\columnwidth minus .5\columnwidth}
   \llap{\em a difficult integral}
\]
```

The second example, with the equation centered between the tags, is produced by

```
\[ \Longrightarrow
   \hspace{.5\columnwidth minus .5\columnwidth}
      g(x)=\int_a^b dx\, \frac{f(x)}{\sqrt{1-x^2}}
   \hspace{.5\columnwidth minus .5\columnwidth}
   \mbox{\em a difficult integral}
\]
```

4.11   Multiletter Variables in Math Mode

LaTeX uses the math italics font for variables in a math environment; for example, `$f(x)$` is typeset as $f(x)$. More importantly, LaTeX treats adjacent letters as different variables multiplied together. This can produce ugly results when a multiletter variable is used. For example, suppose you want to define a symbol for a variable called "Working-Level-Month—effective." The natural `$WLM_{eff}$` produces the strangely spaced result WLM_{eff}. What needs to be done is to use regular italics font. Thus, to produce the more pleasing result WLM_{eff}, you would use `${\em WLM}_{\!\!\em eff}$`. Notice the use of negative spaces `\!` to move the superscript closer to the variable name. If this variable is to be used many times in your document, it is a good idea to define a command to produce this variable by placing in the preamble

```
\newcommand{\WLMeff}{{\em WLM}_{\!\!\em eff}}.
```

Then `$\WLMeff$` will produce WLM_{eff}.

4.12   Roman Font in Math Mode

Often roman font and not italic font is needed in the math environment such as when typing chemical equations. For example, `$$C + H_2 \rightarrow CH_4$$`

produces the unattractive

$$C + 2H_2 \rightarrow CH_4$$

The chemical symbols should be in roman font, and CH is not two separate variables multiplied together. To produce a better result, use

```
$$ \mbox{C} + \mbox{2H_2} \rightarrow \mbox{CH_4}$$
```

to produce

$$C + 2H_2 \rightarrow CH_4$$

As an alternative to using `\mbox{\rm `*roman text*` }`, you can define a `\chem` command to cause all characters to be roman. The `\chem` command is defined in the preamble as

```
\def\chem{\everymath={\fam0 }\fam0 }
```

Note the space after each `\fam0` command. Then, in math mode, the command `\chem` will cause all lettering to be in roman font. For example,

```
$$\chem C + 2H_2 \rightarrow CH_4$$
```

produces

$$C + 2H_2 \rightarrow CH_4$$

Alternatively, if the command `\everymath={\fam0 }` is placed in the preamble of a document, all math will be typeset in roman face.

4.13   Boldface in Math Mode

Math italic is the default font in math mode. In this mode, the `\bf` command causes all uppercase Greek letters and numbers to be printed in boldface. Also, the alphabetic characters are changed from math italics to bold Roman font. However, in math mode, lower case Greek letters and all operators are treated as symbols, and are thus unaffected by the command `\bf`. Consider the following example.

$a A \omega \Omega \simeq\equiv 4.5$ `$ a A \omega \Omega \simeq \equiv 4.5 $`

$\mathbf{a A} \omega \Omega \simeq\equiv \mathbf{4.5}$ `$ \bf a A \omega \Omega \simeq \equiv 4.5 $`

To create bold lowercase Greek letters, operators, and ***bold math italics***, you must use the `\boldmath` command *before* entering the math mode. The command `\boldmath` causes uppercase Greek letters to be set in bold italics and numbers to become large bold subscripts. Here is how `\boldmath` affects the preceding example.

$\boldsymbol{a A \omega \Omega \simeq\equiv 4.5}$ `{\boldmath $a A \omega`
                                         `\Omega \simeq \equiv 4.5$}`

Because \boldmath is a text mode command, its use becomes rather cumbersome in the displayed math environment where you have to do things like

```
\[ \mbox{\boldmath $\sigma$} = \mbox{\boldmath $\alpha$}
                                - \mbox{\bf b} \]
```

to produce

$$\boldsymbol{\sigma} = \boldsymbol{\alpha} - \mathbf{b}$$

Here is a preamble macro for use in math mode that will produce the appropriate boldface (either \boldmath or \bf) for any symbol:

```
\newcommand{\mathbold}[1]{\mbox{\boldmath $\bf#1$}}
```

With this macro, the example equation can be composed more easily as

```
\[ \mathbold{ \sigma = \alpha - b} \]
```

4.13.1   Accents in Boldmath

As explained above, to obtain a bold lowercase Greek letter it is necessary to use \boldmath; for example, to produce μ you enter $\mbox{\boldmath μ}$. However, to put an accent on such a lowercase Greek letter is not so easy. There is a warning on page 201 of Lamport's book that \boldmath may have problems, but it does not mention accents. Apparently, some accents cause \boldmath great problems. For example, $\mbox{\boldmath $\hat{\mu}$}$ produces $\hat{\boldsymbol\mu}$, which gives an accent that looks like a smile going through the μ.

However, \widehat does not cause such problems. To produce $\widehat{\boldsymbol\mu}$, you enter

```
$\mbox{\boldmath $\widehat\mu$}$.
```

To produce a regular size, but not bold, hat symbol on a bold μ, that is, $\hat{\boldsymbol\mu}$ requires an equally awkward sequence:

```
$\hat{\mbox{\boldmath $\mu$}}$
```

4.14   A Better Dot Product Operator

The \cdot in math mode for the dot product operator is too small, as in $\mathbf{U} \cdot \mathbf{V}$ ($\bf U \cdot V$) and the \bullet symbol produces too large a dot, as in $\mathbf{U} \bullet \mathbf{V}$ ($\bf U \bullet V$). Moreover, the spacing around the dot is a bit large. Here are two alternatives that differ only in their spacing around the dot:

$\mathbf{U} \cdot \mathbf{V}$ from `$\bf U \!\stackrel{\scriptscriptstyle\bullet}{{}}\! V$`
$\mathbf{U} \cdot \mathbf{V}$ from `$\bf U {\scriptscriptstyle \stackrel{\bullet}{{}}} V$`.

To use one of these alternatives, it is best to define a `\dotprod` command in the preamble with, for example,

`\newcommand{\dotprod}{{\scriptscriptstyle \stackrel{\bullet}{{}}}}`

Then, to produce **U•V**, simply type `$\bf U \dotprod V$`.

4.15   Two Compound Math Operators

In many math documents the "greater than or approximately equal to" ($\gtrsim$) or the "less than or approximately equal to" ($\lesssim$) operators are needed. However, LaTeX does not include these compound operators in its fonts (although they are included in the $\mathcal{AMS}$-LaTeX fonts under the NFSS). These two operators can be constructed by placing the following in your preamble.

```
\makeatletter
%------- Compound Math Operators by D. Arseneau
\def\gsim{\compoundrel>\over\sim}
\def\lsim{\compoundrel<\over\sim}
\def\compoundrel#1\over#2{\mathpalette\compoundreL{{#1}\over{#2}}}
\def\compoundreL#1#2{\compoundREL#1#2}
\def\compoundREL#1#2\over#3{\mathrel
     {\vcenter{\hbox{$\m@th\buildrel{#1#2}\over{#1#3}$}}}}
\makeatother
```

Then use `$\gsim$` to produce $\gtrsim$ and `$\lsim$` to produce $\lesssim$.

4.16   Matrix Expressions

LaTeX's `array` environment can be used to create matrix equations, as shown in the following example:

$$\left(\begin{array}{ccc} a & b & c \\ d & e & f \\ g & h & i \end{array} \right) \left(\begin{array}{c} x \\ y \\ z \end{array} \right) = \left(\begin{array}{c} \alpha \\ \beta \\ \gamma \end{array} \right)$$

```
\left( \begin{array}{ccc}
      a & b & c \\
      d & e & f \\
      g & h & i
      \end{array} \right)
\left( \begin{array}{c}
      x \\ y \\ z
      \end{array}  \right) =
\left( \begin{array}{c}
      \alpha \\ \beta \\ \gamma
      \end{array}  \right)
```

If you use parentheses to delimit the arrays (as in this example), it is easier to use TEX's \pmatrix command as in

$$
\begin{pmatrix} a & b & c \\ d & e & f \\ g & h & i \end{pmatrix}
\begin{pmatrix} x \\ y \\ z \end{pmatrix} =
\begin{pmatrix} \alpha \\ \beta \\ \gamma \end{pmatrix}
$$

```
\pmatrix{a & b & c \cr
         d & e & f \cr
         g & h & i \cr}
\pmatrix{x \cr y \cr z \cr} =
\pmatrix{\alpha \cr \beta \cr
                     \gamma \cr}
```

TEX's \vphantom command can also be used to give vertical alignment of a row vector times a matrix. Consider these two cases:

$$
(x \quad y \quad z)
\begin{pmatrix} a & b & c \\ d & e & f \\ g & h & i \end{pmatrix}
$$

```
\pmatrix{x & y & z\cr}
\pmatrix{a & b & c \cr
         d & e & f \cr
         g & h & i \cr}
```

$$
(x \quad y \quad z)
\begin{pmatrix} a & b & c \\ d & e & f \\ g & h & i \end{pmatrix}
$$

```
\matrix{ \pmatrix{x & y & z\cr} \cr
         \vphantom{ 0 } \cr
         \vphantom{ 0 } \cr}
\pmatrix{a & b & c \cr
         d & e & f \cr
         g & h & i \cr}
```

4.17   Continued Fractions

A continued fraction such as

$$
t_0 + \cfrac{1}{t_1 + \cfrac{1}{t_2 + \cfrac{1}{t_3 + \cfrac{1}{t_4 + \cdots}}}}
$$

is created by

```
\[
 t_0+\frac{1}{t_1+\frac{\textstyle 1}
  {\textstyle t_2+\frac{\textstyle 1}
  {\textstyle t_3+\frac{\textstyle 1}
  {\textstyle t_4+\cdots}}}}
\]
```

A continued fraction can also be written in "short" form as

$$
1 + \frac{1}{\lceil t_1} + \frac{1}{\lceil t_2} + \frac{1}{\lceil t_3} + \frac{1}{\lceil t_4} + \cdots,
$$

by the following input

```
$$1+\cfrac{1}{t_1}+\cfrac{1}{t_2}+\cfrac{1}{t_3}+
              \cfrac{1}{t_4}+\cdots ,$$
```

To use this short form, you must first define the following definition of `\cfrac` in the preamble.

```
\def\cfrac#1#2{\array{c}\multicolumn{1}{c|}{#1}\\
              \hline\multicolumn{1}{|c}{#2}\endarray}
```

4.18   Chemical Reaction Arrows

To produce a chemical reaction equation such as

$$A + B \underset{k_2}{\overset{k_1}{\rightleftharpoons}} C$$

a double-arrow reaction rate symbol is needed. One method is to define in the preamble the macro

```
\def\reactionrates#1#2{\mathrel{\mathop{\rightleftharpoons}\limits^{#1}_{#2}}}
```

and then use

```
\mbox{A} + \mbox{B} \reactionrates{k_1}{k_2} \mbox{C}
```

4.19   Placing Frames around Equations

Sometimes you will want to emphasize an equation by placing a box or frame around it, such as $\boxed{x^2 = z + \sin(z)}$ or even

$$\boxed{f(x,y) = x^2 + y^2}$$

To produce this, use

```
... equations such as \framebox{$x^2 = z + \sin(z)$} or even
{\fboxsep=.2in
$$  \framebox{$ f(x,y) = x^2 + y^2 $} $$ }
```

To add equation numbers to a boxed equation is a bit more complex. To produce

$$\boxed{f(x,y) = x^2 + y^2}$$

(4.10)

use the following:

```
\begin{equation}
    \mbox{\fboxsep=.1in \framebox{$ f(x,y) = x^2 + y^2 $}}
\end{equation}
```

Putting a box around multiline equations is more difficult. The easiest way is to use the TABLE macros (see Section 5.4). To produce

$$\boxed{\begin{aligned}
\frac{dP(t)}{dt} &= \frac{\rho - \bar{\beta}}{\ell} P(t) + \sum_{i=1}^{G} \lambda_i C_i(t) + S(t) \\
\frac{dC_i(t)}{dt} &= -\lambda_i C_i(t) + \frac{\bar{\beta}_i}{\ell} P(t), \qquad i = 1, \ldots, G
\end{aligned}}$$

(4.11)

use the following (it is assumed that the TABLE macros have been loaded):

```
\begin{equation}
\BeginTable
 \OpenUp99
 \BeginFormat
 |  r M oO | \M        |
 \EndFormat
  \_
 | \frac{dP(t)}{dt} " =  \frac{\rho-\bar{\beta}}{\ell} P(t)
            + \sum_{i=1}^G \lambda_i C_i(t) + S(t) | \\+44
 | \frac{d C_i(t)}{dt} " = -\lambda_i C_i(t)
 + \frac{\bar{\beta}_i}{\ell} P(t), \qquad i=1,\ldots,G  | \\+44
  \_
\EndTable
\end{equation}
```

To avoid automatic generation of equation numbers, replace the `\begin{equation}` ... `\end{equation}` by $$ ... $$.

4.20   Word Equations in Boxes

Sometimes you may want to use word equations, that is, blocks of text in boxes. For example,

$$
\boxed{\begin{array}{c}\text{The Total Document or}\\ \text{Great Big Book Made}\\ \text{from Many Parts}\end{array}} \;=\; \boxed{\text{Part 1}} \;+\; \cdots \;+\; \boxed{\text{Part n}}
$$

$$(4.12)$$

This was produced with

```
\begin{equation}
 \mbox{\framebox{\parbox{1.5in}{\centering
 The Total Document or Great Big Book Made from Many Parts}} \ = \ %
 \framebox{\parbox{1.0in}{\centering Part 1}} \ + $\cdots$ + \ %
 \framebox{\parbox{1.0in}{\centering Part n}}}
\end{equation}
```

4.21   Math in Section Titles

You must be careful when placing math, references, and citations in the title of a chapter, section, subsection, or the like. If special care is not taken you will encounter the dreaded error message "`TeX capacity exceeded, sorry...`". For example, the statement

```
\subsubsection*{Solution of Equation \boldmath $y''(x) = f(x)$}
```

will cause just such a problem no matter what the capacity of your TeX compiler. Remember, the commands \section, \subsection, and so on, have *moving* arguments (the argument appears as a heading as well as in the .toc file), and fragile commands in such an argument must be "protected." Commands like \boldmath, \cite, and \ref must be protected with the \protect command. For example, to produce the title

Solution of Equation $y''(x) = f(x)$

you must use

```
\subsubsection*{Solution of Equation \protect\boldmath $y''(x) = f(x)$}.
```

Chapter 5

Tables

Tables are prominent features of many technical documents. LaTeX provides two environments for typesetting tabular data. The first, the `tabbing` environment, is appropriate for simple tables. The second, the `tabular` environment, is designed for producing more elaborate tables. However, to create very complex tables, it is best to employ special sets of macros. One such set, Michael Wichura's TABLE macros, is highly recommended for producing tables that have many intricate formatting requirements. All three of these methods for producing tables are summarized in this chapter.

5.1   Types of Tables

Tables can either be positioned in the main text where they are defined or created as floating objects. Except for very small tables, it is generally better to place a table in the floating `table` environment in order to allow LaTeX to pick the best position for the table and also to allow LaTeX to create the table caption and table number. The left example below shows the structure used for a typical fixed-position table, while the right example is for a typical floating table. Both examples use the `tabular` environment to define the table contents.

```
%-- A fixed position table           %-- A floating table
\begin{center}                        \begin{table}[htbp]
    table title                          \centering
  \begin{tabular}{...}                   \caption{...}\label{...}
    table definition                     \begin{tabular}{...}
  \end{tabular}                            table definition
\end{center}                             \end{tabular}
                                      \end{table}
```

5.1.1   Captions and Reference Labels

In the floating `table` environment, the `\caption` command is used to place a caption next to the table (usually above it). The form of this command is

$$\texttt{\textbackslash caption}[\textit{list-of-tables-entry}]\{\textit{caption-text}\}$$

where the optional *list-of-tables-entry* is an alternative caption for the list of tables (`.LOT` file), and *caption-text* is the caption to be placed over the table. LaTeX affixes to this table caption a label such as "Table 5.12:"; the number is the table number that is automatically generated by LaTeX. The `\caption` command cannot be used outside the `table` (or `figure`) floating environment.

A reference label may be attached to the caption with the `\label` command. This command must come immediately after the `\caption` command or even be placed inside the `\caption`'s argument to be safe. For example, you might use

```
\caption{The refined results from ...}\label{tblresults}
```

or

```
\caption{The refined results from ... \label{tblresults}}
```

Then, to refer to this table in the text, you would enter something like

```
...the results in Table~\ref{tblresults} were obtained...
```

5.2   The `tabbing` Environment

The `tabbing` environment, invoked by `\begin{tabbing}` ... `\end(tabbing}`, is modeled after tabs on a typewriter, although there are important differences. Data are entered row by row, each terminated by a `\\` or `\kill` command. Within each row, data are separated by `tabbing` environment commands. As with a typewriter, you set tabs (`\=`) or move to the next tab (`\>`).

This environment can be used only in normal text mode, and it creates a single paragraph that LaTeX can break across a page. All formatting (spacing) is determined by the user, and the available formatting features are rather limited. For example, lines (rules) are not easily incorporated. By contrast, the more robust `\tabular` environment can be used in any mode, although it generates a block of output that cannot be broken across a page. The commands available in the `tabbing` environment are given in the accompanying table.

Commands for the `tabbing` Environment

Command	*Purpose*
\=	Sets a tab at the current position and increases the tab counter. Note, tabs are set in the order in which they are entered and *not* in a left-to-right order across the page, since negative \hspace commands can cause the current position to be to the left of a previously used tab stop.
\>	Moves to the next tab. Note that, unlike a typewriter, this command does not always move to the right if the tabs have not been set in left-to-right order.
\\	Starts a new line and resets the next tab position counter to 0.
\kill	Throws away the current line but retains any tab setting made in the line. Starts a new line.
\+	Indents the left margin by one tab stop (equivalent to adding a \> at the start of the next row). Multiple \+ commands are cumulative.
\-	Outdents the left margin by one tab stop. In effect, this command cancels the effect of a previous \+ command.
\<	Used only at the beginning of a row to temporarily outdent by one tab stop for that line, thereby canceling for that line the effect of a previous \+ command.
\'	Used only as the last tab command before the \\ to cause the remaining text to be printed flush right against the right margin.
\'	Causes the text to flow back into the previous column by left justifying any following text against the left tab stop.
\pushtabs	Saves the current position of all tab stops.
\poptabs	Restores the tab positions saved by a previous \pushtabs command.

5.2.1   An Instructional Example

Table 5.1 is an ugly example of the use of the `tabbing` environment, but it demonstrates the use of all the `tabbing` commands. Studying this table reveals several important features of the `tabbing` environment and its commands.

- The \kill command is most often used after the first row of a table to set the scale or distance between tab stops. Rather than use fixed distances, as in this example, you could also enter a dummy row with the longest expected entry for each column used to separate the tab stops.

Table 5.1: An example table, produced in the `tabbing` environment, that illustrates the use of the `tabbing` commands

row	column 1	column 2	column 3	column 4	
1.	aaaa	bbbb	cccc	dddd	
2.	very long first item	*An overlapping second item – beware*			
3.	aaaa	bbbb	cc cc	dddd	outdent to right
4.		aaaa bbbb cccc dddd eeee			
5.		a b c d e			
	6.	a b c d			
	7.	a b c d			
8.		a b c			
9.	aaaa	bbbb	cccc	dddd	back to old tabs

This example was produced with

```
\hrule{}  \vspace{-.2in}
\begin{tabbing}
%% ------------------- Set tab stops
\hspace*{.25in} \= \hspace*{1in} \= \hspace*{1in} \=
                            \hspace*{1in} \= \hspace*{1in} \kill
%% ------------------- Construct Table
%%--create table headings
row \> column 1 \> column 2 \> column 3 \> column 4 \\[.1in]%%--extra space
1.  \> aaaa     \> bbbb    \> cccc    \> dddd     \\
%%--example of overlapping columns
2.  \> very long first item \> {\sl An overlapping second item -- beware} \\
3.  \> aaaa     \> bbbb    \> cc\'cc   \> dddd \' outdent to right \\
    \pushtabs                  %%-- save tab stops
4.  \> \> aaaa \= bbbb \= cccc \= dddd \= eeee \= \\   %%--set new tabs
5.  \>    \> a \> b \> c \> d \> e  \+ \+ \\   %%--move in left margin
6.  \> a \> b \> c \> d  \\
\<7.\> a \> b \> c \> d \- \- \\   %%--shift left and restore left margin
8.  \>    \> a \> b \> c  \\       %%--back to normal left margin
    \poptabs                   %%-- restore tab stops
9.\> aaaa      \> bbbb \> cccc \> dddd \' back to old tabs \\
\end{tabbing} \vspace{-.2in}  \hrule{}
```

- Row 2 illustrates that \> does not behave like a typewriter's tab key. \> places the current position at the next tab stop *in the numerical order in which the stops were defined.* It does *not* move the current position to the tab immediately to the right of the last entry. Thus, for entries that overflow a column's width, you will get overlapping of the text, as in this example.

- Row 3 illustrates how \' is used to shift text to the left and how \` shifts the last entry all the way to the right page margin.

- After the tab positions are saved, rows 4 and 5 show how new tabs stops can be inserted between old tab stops. The \+\+ in row 5 also shifts the left margin in two tab stops for all subsequent lines.

- Row 7 shows how \< is used to move left by one tab stop and how \-\- is used to move the left margin for subsequent lines to the left by two tab stops.

- After \poptabs restores the old tab stops (saved by \pushtabs), row 9 is printed like row 1. The \pushtabs and \poptabs must always be used in nested pairs.

5.3   The `tabular` Environment

To create a table in the `tabular` environment, the table definition is placed between the pair of commands

> \begin{tabular}[*position*]{*format*} ... \end{tabular}

The two parameters of the `tabular` environment are (1) *position*, an optional argument that indicates the vertical position of the tabular with respect to the preceding text (either top [t] or bottom [b]), and (2) *format*, which the number of columns and how items are to be positioned in each column. Without the optional [*position*] argument, the tabular is centered vertically on the current text line. Here are some examples of the *format* parameter.

{lcr}   three columns with the first entry left justified, the second centered, and the third right justified

{|lcr|}   same as the preceding with vertical rules to the left of the first column and to the right of the third column

`{|1 p{4.5cm} rr|}`	four columns; the second is in paragraph mode 4.5 cm wide; vertical rules to the left of the first column and to the right of the fourth
`{c r@{--}l}`	three columns; the first centered, the second right justified, and the third left justified; between columns 2 and 3 characters `--` are placed and the `@` indicated the normal intercolumn space between columns 2 and 3 is to be suppressed

Within the `tabular` environment, the following commands are used to construct a table.

Commands Used in the `tabular` Environment

Command	*Purpose*
`&`	Used to separate column entries.
`\\[`*vshift*`]`	Denotes a row end with an optional vertical space of *vshift* (for example, `[.25in]`) before the next row.
`\hline`	Draws a horizontal line across all columns.
`\vline`	Draws a vertical line over a row's full height and depth.
`\cline{n-m}`	Draws a horizontal line across columns n through m.
`\multicolumn{#1}{#2}{#3}`	Places a multicolumn heading. There are three arguments: `#1=`*nn* to place the heading over next *nn* columns; `#2` the format for the heading, for example, `{|c|}`; `#3` is the text for the heading
`\rule{0in}{`*vshift*`}`	A strut to make the current row have a height of *vshift* (for example, `{3ex}`). Place this next to one of the column entries to produce extra vertical space above the row.

Table 5.2 was constructed with all these commands. Of special note in this table are the methods used to insert vertical space between rows and around the horizontal rules. The optional argument of the `\\` command, for example, `\\[.5ex]`, is used to insert vertical space below the current row. To increase space above the current row, a strut is added. Since several struts are used in this table, a strut command `\STRUT` is defined by

$$\texttt{\\newcommand\{\\STRUT\}\{\\rule\{0in\}\{3ex\}\}}$$

and then used in any row for which extra space above the row is desired.

Table 5.2: An example table, produced in the `tabular` environment, that illustrates the use of all the `tabular` commands

Extreme Ranges of Thermal Conductivities at 273 K		
Material	k (W m^{-1} K^{-1})	*Comment*
hydrogen	0.175	highest for gases
chloroform	0.0066	low for gases
mercury	8.21	high for liquids
freon	0.0228	low for liquids
silver	418.0	high for solids
pyrex glass	1.05	low for solids

This table was produced with

```
%------------------ Example Figure
\begin{center} \footnotesize
\newcommand{\STRUT}{\rule{0in}{3ex}}        %%--- Define a strut
\begin{tabular}{|l r@{.}l |p{1.0in}|}       %%--- Set table format
    %------------------ Top Block Headings
    \hline
    \multicolumn{4}{|c|}
        {\small \bf Extreme Ranges of Thermal \STRUT} \\[1.5ex]
    \multicolumn{4}{|c|}
        {\small \bf Conductivities at 273~K} \\[1.3ex]
    \hline \hline
    %------------------ Table Column Headings
    {\em Material} \hspace{.2in} \vline &
        \multicolumn{2}{c}{$k$ (W m$^{-1}$ K$^{-1}$)} &
        {\em Comment} \STRUT \\[1ex]    \hline
    %------------------ Table Contents
    hydrogen\STRUT    & 0&175  & highest for gases \\
    chloroform        & 0&0066 & low for gases        \\ \cline{4-4}
    mercury           & 8&21   & high for liquids  \\
    freon             & 0&0228 & low for liquids    \\ \cline{4-4}
    silver            & 418&0  & high for solids   \\
    pyrex glass &\hspace{.25in} 1&05   & low for solids\\[1.3ex]
    \hline
\end{tabular} \normalsize \end{center}
```

5.3.1 Aligning Numbers on the Decimal Point

Aligning numbers in the `tabular` environment on the decimal point (some of which may have no decimal point) can be done in several ways. To produce

Case	Numbers Aligned on Decimal
a	245.245
b	1.05
c	0.00012345
d	12,000
e	5

the easiest way may be to use the following:

```
\begin{center} \begin{tabular}{|cr@{}c@{}l@{}|}
\hline
 Case & \multicolumn{3}{c|}{Numbers Aligned on Decimal} \\
\hline
a &  \hspace{0.5in} 245&.&245      \\
b &  1&.&05          \\
c &  0&.&00012345 \\
d &  12,000& &      \\
e &  5&    &        \\
\hline
\end{tabular} \end{center}
```

5.3.2 Vertical Alignment of Tables Headings

In many tables with multiline column headers, the text for some headers needs to be displaced half a line downwards, such as in headers for the first and last columns in the following example.

Material	Parameter		Error
	α	β	
Aluminum	0.23	18.2	15.1%
Magnesium	0.44	14.3	18.2%
Iron	0.75	12.9	25.0%

First define in the preamble the following new command

```
\newcommand{\Lower}[1]{\smash{\lower 1.5ex \hbox{#1}}}
```

Then use \Lower{*col. header*} to shift *col. header* downward by half a line. The above example was created with

```
\begin{tabular}{|lccc|}
\hline
\Lower{Material}& \multicolumn{2}{c}{Parameter}& \Lower{Error}\\ \cline{2-3}
         &  $\alpha$  &  $\beta$  &           \\ \hline
Aluminum  &  0.23  &  18.2  &  15.1\%  \\
Magnesium &  0.44  &  14.3  &  18.2\%  \\
Iron      &  0.75  &  12.9  &  25.0\%  \\ \hline
\end{tabular}
```

5.3.3   A Simple Floating Table Example

Table 5.3 is an example of a simple floating table produced by the following input.

```
\begin{table}[htbp]
  \centering
    \caption{A simple test table}\label{tst1a}
    \begin{tabular}{|rc|rc|}  \hline
      $i$  &  $E_i$  & $i$  &  $E_i$  \\ \hline
       1   &  0.02   &  6   &  0.1    \\
       2   &  0.03   &  7   &  0.2    \\
       3   &  0.04   &  8   &  0.4    \\
       4   &  0.06   &  9   &  0.7    \\
       5   &  0.08   & 10   &  1.0    \\ \hline
    \end{tabular}
\end{table}
```

Table 5.3: A simple test table

i	E_i	i	E_i
1	0.02	6	0.1
2	0.03	7	0.2
3	0.04	8	0.4
4	0.06	9	0.7
5	0.08	10	1.0

Although simple to define, Table 5.3 has several shortcomings. First, the spacing between the caption and the table is far from ideal, and there is too little space around the horizontal rules. Moreover, if the caption were very long, it would be printed on several lines extending across the full width of the page.

Table 5.4 is a refinement of this table with a longer caption. Notice the use of a \parbox to restrict the width of the table caption and the use of struts and

\vspace commands to improve the vertical spacing. It was produced with the following input.

```
\begin{table}[htbp]
  \begin{center}
  \parbox{3in}{\caption{The discrete energies $E_i$ (MeV) used for
              deriving the approximate line-beam response
              function}\label{tst1b}}

    \vspace{.1in}
    \begin{tabular}{|rc|rc|}  \hline
      $i$  &  $E_i$   & $i$  &  $E_i$ \rule{0in}{3ex} \\[1ex]  \hline
       1   &  0.02    & 6    &
                        \rule{0in}{3ex} 0.1 \rule{0in}{3ex}  \\
       2   &  0.03    & 7    &  0.2   \\
       3   &  0.04    & 8    &  0.4   \\
       4   &  0.06    & 9    &  0.7   \\
       5   &  0.08    & 10   &  1.0   \\[1ex]  \hline
    \end{tabular}
  \end{center}
\end{table}
```

Table 5.4: The discrete energies E_i (MeV) used for deriving the approximate line-beam response function

i	E_i	i	E_i
1	0.02	6	0.1
2	0.03	7	0.2
3	0.04	8	0.4
4	0.06	9	0.7
5	0.08	10	1.0

5.3.4   Tables in a Minipage

A minipage is ideally suited for tables. Not only can the caption size be constrained by the width of the minipage, but footnotes for the table can be treated as footnotes for the minipage. Moreover, footnote symbols in a minipage are letters a, b, c..., just what is needed for a table. An example is shown in Table 5.5, which was produced by the following input:

```
\begin{table}[htb]
\begin{center}
  \begin{minipage}{2.65in}
    \renewcommand{\footnoterule}{}
    \begin{center}
      \caption{A test table with footnotes that was
          created in a minipage environment} \label{minitab}
      \vspace{.1in}
      \begin{tabular}{|rrrrrrrr|} \hline
        \multicolumn{8}{|c|}{\bf Number of Observed Gnarls%
            \footnote{An exotic bug found in \LaTeX\ documents}} \\
        \hline
        102   & 54 & 67 & 5  & 27 & 73 &  35 & 17  \\
        57\footnote{Smith 1993: 1--3001}
              & 38 & 40 & 45 & 38 & 54 & 136 & 357 \\
        39    & 12 & 11 & 55 & 22 & 0  & 41  & 18  \\ \hline
      \end{tabular} \vspace{-.1in}
    \end{center}
  \end{minipage}
\end{center}
\end{table}
```

Table 5.5: A test table with footnotes that was created in a minipage environment

Number of Observed Gnarls[a]							
102	54	67	5	27	73	35	17
57[b]	38	40	45	38	54	136	357
39	12	11	55	22	0	41	18

[a] An exotic bug found in LaTeX documents
[b] Smith 1993: 1–3001

Several things should be noted about Table 5.5. First, the **\footnoterule{}** statement turns off the rule usually placed above footnotes. Without this there would be two lines above the footnotes (the table frame and the footnote rule). Second, two nested centering environments are used, one to center the minipage and the other to center the table in the minipage. Third, two **\vspace** adjustments are made above and below the table frame to position the caption and footnotes correctly. Finally, it is important to pick the width of the minipage correctly so as to have the correct horizontal placement of the footnotes.

To simplify the construction of a table in a minipage, place the following environment definition in the preamble.

```
%-------- A Minipage Table Environment
\newenvironment{mptbl}{\begin{center}}{\end{center}}
\newenvironment{minipagetbl}[1]
  {\begin{center}\begin{minipage}{#1}
     \renewcommand{\footnoterule}{} \begin{mptbl}}%
  {\vspace{-.1in} \end{mptbl} \end{minipage} \end{center}}
```

With this `minipagetbl` environment, Table 5.5 can be constructed more compactly as

```
\begin{table}[htbp]
  \begin{minipagetbl}{2.65in}
    \caption{A test table ... }\label{minitab} \vspace{.1in}
    \begin{tabular}{|rrrrrrrr|} \hline
          . . . . . .
    \end{tabular}
  \end{minipagetbl}
\end{table}
```

5.3.5 Side-by-Side Tables

You can use two side-by-side `minipage` environments to place two tables side by side on the page. By placing both `minipages` in a `table` environment, the twin tables can be made into a single floating object. Here is an example.

Table 5.6: The discrete energies E_i (MeV) used to calculate the approximation

i	E_i	i	E_i
1	0.02	4	0.1
2	0.03	5	0.2
3	0.04	6	0.4

Table 5.7: Another set of data for E_i (MeV) used to calculate the approximation

i	E_i	i	E_i
1	0.05	4	1.0
2	0.08	5	2.0
3	0.12	6	5.0

These side-by-side tables were produced with the following

```
\begin{table}[htbp]
\begin{minipage}[t]{2.30in}
  \centering
  \parbox[t]{2.00in}{\caption{The discrete energies $E_i$ (MeV) used to
          calculate the approximation}\label{twin1}} \\ \vspace{.1in}
  \begin{tabular}{|rc|rc|}  \hline
       $i$  &  $E_i$  & $i$  & $E_i$ \\  \hline
```

```
           1  &  0.02   &  4  &  0.1   \\
           2  &  0.03   &  5  &  0.2   \\
           3  &  0.04   &  6  &  0.4   \\  \hline
        \end{tabular}
     \end{minipage}
  \hfill
  \begin{minipage}[t]{2.30in}
     \centering
     \parbox[t]{2.00in}{\caption{Another set of data for $E_i$ (MeV) used
           to calculate the approximation}\label{twin2}}\\ \vspace{.1in}
     \begin{tabular}{|rc|rc|}  \hline
           $i$  &  $E_i$   &  $i$  &  $E_i$  \\  \hline
           1  &  0.05   &  4  &  1.0   \\
           2  &  0.08   &  5  &  2.0   \\
           3  &  0.12   &  6  &  5.0   \\  \hline
        \end{tabular}
     \end{minipage}
  \end{table}
```

5.3.6 Vertical Alignment of Column Entries

One way to align vertically the row entries in a table is to place each entry in a **tabular** environment. For example

First row	This is a row entry that extends over several lines so that it has a vertical length that is much longer that the first column's entry.	This is a box of text that is only two lines deep.
Second row	This is yet another row entry that extends over several lines, and once again it has a vertical length that is much longer that the first column's entry.	This is a box of text that is only two lines deep.

is produced by

```
  \begin{center}
    \begin{tabular}{|ccc|} \hline
       \begin{tabular}{@{}p{0.8in}@{}}
          First row                                   \end{tabular} &
       \begin{tabular}{@{}p{2in}@{}}
          This is  ... first column's entry.           \end{tabular} &
       \begin{tabular}{@{}p{1.5in}@{}}
```

```
      This is a box ... two lines deep.        \end{tabular}\\[.7in]
    \begin{tabular}{@{}p{0.8in}@{}}
      Second row                               \end{tabular} &
    \begin{tabular}{@{}p{2in}@{}}
      This is yet another ... column's entry.  \end{tabular} &
    \begin{tabular}{@{}p{1.5in}@{}}
      This is a box ... two lines deep.        \end{tabular}\\ \hline
  \end{tabular}
\end{center}
```

5.3.7 Paragraphs in a Box

Sometimes you may want to place a box or frame around some text such as in this example. The trick is to put the text into a minipage (to justify the text) and then place the minipage into a one-column one-entry table (to create the box). With this approach you can even put equations like this into the box.

$$f(x) = \sqrt{1 + x^2} \tag{5.1}$$

To create boxed text like this, put the following macro in the document's preamble.

```
\newlength{\boxedparwidth}        \setlength{\boxedparwidth}{.92\textwidth}
\newenvironment{boxedtext}%
    {\begin{center} \begin{tabular}{|@{\hspace{.15in}}c@{\hspace{.15in}}|}
                \hline \\ \begin{minipage}[t]{\boxedparwidth}
                \setlength{\parindent}{.25in}}%
    {\end{minipage} \\ \\ \hline \end{tabular} \end{center}}
```

The boxed example above was then produced with

```
\begin{boxedtext}  Sometimes you may want ... \end{boxedtext}
```

5.3.8 Controlling Spacing in Tables

Eventually, you will encounter a table that is just a bit too wide for the page. This most often occurs when trying to squeeze a table into a column of a two-column page. Two solutions are offered. First, simply decrease the size of the font used for the table (and hence the table size) by using

```
\begin{table}
    \small %(or \footonotesize or ...)
    \begin{tabular}
        . . .
    \end{tabular}
\end{table}
```

The second, preferred solution is to decrease the intercolumn spacing used in the table. There are several format parameters (see Appendix B) that you can change with the \renewcommand to alter the spacing in your tables.

In particular, the parameter \arraystretch controls the line spacing between rows. The command \renewcommand{\arraystretch}{1.5} will increase row spacing to 1.5 times the normal spacing. The horizontal space between table columns is 2 × \tabcolsep, which can also be changed with the \renewcommand. The width between double vertical or horizontal rules can be changed to 0.1 inch by \renewcommand{\doublerulesep}{.1in}. The width of the rule itself is controlled by the parameter \arrayrulewidth.

5.4   TABLE Macros

Michael Wichura has produced a set of macros called TABLE that provides a table environment whose many formatting features allow the construction of very complex tables. This macro set, contained in the a file called tables.tex, may be freely distributed; however, the 94-page manual with many examples and detailed instructions for using these macros must be purchased from Personal TEX, Inc., 12 Madrona, Mill Valley, CA 94941. These macros allow a great deal of flexibility in formatting a table, and if you have many complex tables to produce, there is no better set of tools.

To use these macros, include \input table in the preamble of your LaTeX file to include these table macros. As with the tabular environment, tables can be created with a caption and a label so that they can be referenced in the text. Table 5.8, which resembles Table 5.4, is produced with

```
\begin{table}[htbp]
\centering
\parbox{3in}{\caption{The discrete energies $E_i$ (MeV) used for
             deriving the approximate line-beam response function}
             \label{tst1}}
$$\BeginTable
    \def\R{\JustRight}     \def\C{\JustCenter}
    \BeginFormat
```

```
  | n2 |   n1.2   | n2 |   n2.1 |
\EndFormat
\_
| i    " \C $E_i$ |  i    " \R $E_i$ | \\+44
\_
| 1    "   0.02   | 6    "   0.1 | \\+40
| 2    "   0.03   | 7    "   0.2 | \\
| 3    "   0.04   | 8    "   0.4 | \\
| 4    "   0.06   | 9    "   0.7 | \\
| 5    "   0.08   | 10   "   1.0 | \\+04
\_
  \EndTable$$
\end{table}
```

Table 5.8: The discrete energies E_i (MeV) used for deriving the approximate line-beam response function

i	E_i	i	E_i
1	0.02	6	0.1
2	0.03	7	0.2
3	0.04	8	0.4
4	0.06	9	0.7
5	0.08	10	1.0

5.4.1 Using the T$_A$B$_L$E Macros

To define a table with the T$_A$B$_L$E macros use, the following structure:

$$\BeginTable
prologue section
format section
data section
\EndTable$$

The initial and final $$ are used to center the table between the left and right margins. Without them, the table is left justified on the page. The trick to using the T$_A$B$_L$E macros is to master the many codes available for the three sections of the table. Following are some of the important commands and codes used; however, many features not presented in this summary are available and are described in the T$_A$B$_L$E manual.

The Prologue Section

The prologue section is used (1) to define shorthand commands for use in the data section, and (2) to specify general spacing and size parameters for the table. Some examples follow.

Useful Commands for the Prologue Section

Command	*Usage*
`\Expand`	Increases intercolumn spacing so that the table fills the entire width of the page
`\LongLine`	Extends `\_` lines across the page (margin to margin)
`\ninepoint`	Uses 9-point fonts for the table
`\OpenUp`nm	Adds n strut units to the height and m strut units to the depth of the usual end of row strut
`\SetTableToWidth{`⟨*dimen*⟩`}`	Stretches or compresses table to a width of ⟨*dimen*⟩
`\WidenTableBy{`⟨*dimen*⟩`}`	Widens table by an amount ⟨*dimen*⟩ (may be positive or negative)
`\def\C{\JustCenter}`	Defines `\C` to center data entry, overriding stipulated format
`\def\L{\JustLeft}`	Defines `\L` to left justify data entry, overriding stipulated format
`\def\R{\JustRight}`	Defines `\R` to right justify data entry, overriding stipulated format
`\def\TXT{`*any text*`}`	`\TXT` in the data section will produce *any text*
`\def\B#1{\beta_{#1}}`	`\B5` in the data section produces β_5; note the use of an argument in this definition

Format Section

The format section for an n column table has the form

```
\BeginFormat
    | ⟨keys₁⟩ | ⟨keys₂⟩ | ··· | ⟨keysₙ⟩ |
\EndFormat
```

or, more compactly,

```
\BeginFormat     | ⟨keys₁⟩ | ⟨keys₂⟩ | ··· | ⟨keysₙ⟩ | .
```

where ⟨$keys_i$⟩ denotes a (possibly empty) string of *format keys*, separated by optional blanks, that succinctly describe the layout of the ith column. The T̲A̲B̲L̲E macros have many format keys for specifying how the data entries are to be written and positioned in their columns. The following table describes some of the more important formatting keys used by TABLE.

Column Formatting Codes

Key Code	Description
*	**Repeat key:** used to repeat a format, for example, `*{n}{c|}` specifies the format `c|` is to be repeated `n` times.
c, l, r	**Alignment Keys:** centers (c), left justifies (l), or right justifies (r) the data entry in the column.
B, T, R, S, I, f	**Font selection keys:** prints data in bold (B), typewriter font (T), roman font (R), slant font (S), italic font (I), or some other user-specified font (`f<font identifier>`), such as `f\sc` for small capitals.
m, M, \m, \M	**Math keys:** sets entries in math mode (m) or display mode (M). The `\m` and `\M` forms are used to get the right half of a math expression to line up on an relational operator (=).
n, N	**Numeric keys:** Causes numeric data to be aligned on their explicit or implicit decimal points. `N` and `n` often give the same results; however `N` uses math mode so that $-$ signs have the same width as $+$ signs. Examples of use are `n[000.00]` or `n3.2`, `N[00000]` or `N5`, and for numbers with exponents, `n[0.0000\times10^{-0.0}]`. NOTE: Use `{}` for an empty entry; no blanks are allowed.
s, o	**Intercolumn space keys:** `s` sets the width of the white space to the right of the current column and all subsequent columns. `o` is like `s` but changes the white space only just to the right of the current column; the preceding `s` spacing is then reinstated. Examples: `s3`, `o0`, `s`, `s(.25in)`.
i, j, k	**Kern keys:** `i` places nonstretchable white space (kern) before each entry, `j` places the kern after the entries, and `k` places the kern before and after each entry. Examples: `i3` and `k(.5cm)`.
w	**Column width key:** Forces the column to be at least as wide as specified. Examples: `w5`, `w(2.5cm)`, and `w[sample entry]`.
p	**Paragraph key:** Sets each entry in "paragraph mode" in a column of a specified width. Examples: `p30` and `p(3in)`. The indentation format of the paragraph can be specified in the prologue by, for example, `\EveryTableParBox={\noindent \hangafter=1 \hangindent=.25in}`.

The Data Section

Part of the table definition specifies the contents of the table as well as how table lines are to be drawn. T$_A$BLE prefers to use single lines, although with effort double lines, dotted lines and the such can be created. A typical data line for a row in a 4-column table might look like this

```
|  $x_1$ "  3.2675 |  $y_3$  "  1.234\times10^{-5}  |  \\+2{-3}
```

Here the | and " are used to separate the data entries (| causes a vertical line to be drawn, and " omits such a line). If a | or " is to be used as part of the entry for a particular column use the special macros \VBar and \DQuote.

Each table row is terminated by a \\. If the spacing above and below the row is to be altered from the default, the \\ can be followed by +*hd* to add *h* and *d* strut units (points) to the height and depth of the normal strut. Here *h* and *d* are positive or negative integers or zero, and the parentheses can be omitted if the number is a single unsigned digit. To prevent any strut at all from being used for a table row, use \\0.

To draw a horizontal line across the table simply place _ between the two table rows where the line is wanted.

Listed on the next page are some commands frequently used in the data section. These commands are used in defining the data entries (that is, those quantitites placed between | or " symbols.

Useful Commands for the Data Section

Command	*Description*
\-	Draws a horizontal line across the width of the column. Usually used in rows terminated by \\0.
\=	Draws a horizontal line across the width of the column and halfway into the adjacent intercolumn spaces. Usually used in rows terminated by \\0.
~	Typesets a nonprinting digit.
\Backspace*d*	Inserts a leading kern of width $-d$ units.
\Center	Centers the entry and uses the rest of the column format.
\DQuote	Typesets the character ".
\Enlarge{H}{D}	Typesets the entry with the column format, but increases the natural height and depth of the result by the dimension $\{H\}$ and $\{D\}$. Example \Enlarge{3pt}{3pt} *data entry.*
\JustCenter	Centers the entry and omits the column format.
\JustLeft	Left justifies the entry and omits the column format.
\JustRight	Right justifies the entry and omits the column format.
\Left	Positions the entry flush left and uses the rest of the column format.
\Lower	Lowers the entry by a specified amount. Examples: \Lower {entry}, \Lower8 {entry}, or \Lower(.5in) {entry}.
\Raise	Raises the entry by a specified amount. Examples: \Raise {entry}, \Raise8 {entry}, or \Raise(.5in) {entry}.
\Right	Positions the entry flush right and uses the rest of the column format.
\Smash	Typesets the entry so as to be centered about the baseline, but declares the height and depth of the result to be zero.
\use{c}	Uses the space of the next c columns and the format of the last of these columns to typeset the entry. Examples: \use4 or \use{12}.
\Use{c}[key]{text}	Uses the next c columns to typeset **text** according to the format specified by **key**.
\VBar	Typesets the character |. Example use: {\tt \VBar}.

Chapter 6

Graphics

Graphs, line drawings, and other pictorial material are an integral part of many technical documents. Yet one of the greatest challenges for LaTeX users is how best to incorporate graphics into their documents since LaTeX has only primitive graphical capabilities. In this chapter, the `picture` environment that LaTeX provides for creating pictures in documents is discussed. Special macro sets and external programs that extend LaTeX's capabilities are also considered. Finally, methods for the preparation and importation of non-LaTeX graphic files into a LaTeX document are presented.

However, before the details are presented about specific methods for inserting graphics into a document, an overview of the various methods will provide the reader with some appreciation of the multiple approaches that can be used and of the need to go beyond standard LaTeX for complex graphics.

6.1 Methods for Including Graphics

Several different approaches can be pursued, and the one that is best for a particular document depends on many factors. Here is a summary of the different methods with their capabilities and limitations.

6.1.1 Cut and Paste

The simplest of all methods for including a graphic into your document is to leave a blank space where you want the graphic and, after printing the document, paste in the graphic that you have created outside LaTeX. For example, a floating figure with a space for a 4-inch-tall graphic (including the space above and below the graphic) is created by

```
\begin{figure}[htbp]
    \vspace{4in}    %%-- space for graphic
    \caption{...}\label{...}
\end{figure}
```

The advantages of this method are that (1) it is the quickest way to produce a LATEX document, (2) almost any method can be used to create the graphic (for example, photographs, CAD programs, or artists), and (3) the LATEX document remains independent of hardware and the LATEX implementation (that is, the LATEX file is portable, albeit without the graphics included). The main disadvantage of this approach is the extra work needed to paste the graphics into the document. This can be quite burdensome if many revisions of the document are required.

6.1.2 Use the `picture` Environment

Although LATEX was not designed to generate graphical material, it does have a rudimentary capability for producing line drawings. The `picture` environment allows you to create simple pictures composed of lines, arrows, boxes, circles, bezier curves, and horizontal text. In Section 6.2, the various commands available in the `picture` environment are summarized and illustrated. However, this approach for including graphics in your document is restricted to fairly simple drawings.

The advantages of the `picture` environment are that (1) graphics become an integral part of your document, (2) it creates a source file that can be used with any LATEX implementation (that is, your document is portable), (3) the text used for labels in the picture will be in the same font style as that used for the document text, and (4) the drawings can be previewed on the screen.

The disadvantages are that (1) it requires considerable effort to create a complex figure, usually requiring you first to draw the figure on graph paper and then to enter many (x, y) coordinates for each element (line, circle, label, and the like) of the picture, (2) lines can be draw only with a finite number of different slopes, and (3) all text labels are horizontal (for example, text cannot be turned sideways to label the y-axis of an x-y graph).

6.1.3 Extend LATEX's `picture` Capabilities

Several sets of macros have been developed to extend the capabilities of the `picture` environment. Two popular sets are the EPIC/EEPIC and the PICTEX macro collections. These macro sets allow you to use many more line styles with different widths and any slope, to include many more shapes and symbols in the pictures, and to construct *x-y* and bar graphs much more easily. Graphic macro packages are briefly discussed in Section 6.3.

The advantages of using such graphic macro packages are that (1) line drawings for all but the most complicated figures can be created, (2) the figures become an integral part of your document and can be previewed, and (3) the source file is portable (provided the special macro sets are also provided). The disadvantages are that (1) you need to procure these macro sets since they are not part of LaTeX, (2) considerable effort is still required to create a complex picture or graph, (3) large or complex pictures will often exhaust LaTeX's memory, and (4) text labels are still printed only horizontally.

6.1.4   Use Other Programs to Generate LaTeX Pictures

A principal disadvantage of LaTeX's `picture` environment, even when supplemented by special macro sets like PiCTeX, is the relatively large effort required to produce a picture. The coordinates of each element in the figure must be painstakingly calculated and entered. Many iterations are often required before a satisfactory finished picture is created. As an alternative, several programs, such as GnuPlot, TeXCAD, and xfig, are available that allow you to compose a picture or graph much more easily. These programs can then produce a LaTeX file composed of `picture` environment commands (plus, optionally, commands from EEPIC/EPIC or other special macro packages). This file can then be included directly into your LaTeX document with the `\input` command (see Section 6.4.1).

Although this method for creating figures greatly facilitates the creation of pictures for inclusion in your LaTeX document, it has the same limitations of the more manual method for creating pictures directly in the `picture` environment.

6.1.5   Use Non-LaTeX Graphics

To avoid the limitations of the (extended) `picture` environment, an entirely different approach for including graphics in a LaTeX document is to create outside LaTeX the graphic image in some robust graphics language (for example, PostScript or HPGL[1]). The resulting graphic is first converted (if necessary) into a form that can used by your printer (e.g., PostScript or PCL[2] format) and stored in a file. This graphic file (which LaTeX cannot understand) is then "tied" to your document so

---

[1] An acronym for Hewlett-Packard Graphics Language.
[2] An acronym for Printer Control Language.

that, when your document is printed, the graphic will also be printed. In effect, this approach is just an electronic form of the cut-and-paste approach.

To incorporate such non-LaTeX files into your document, you use TeX's \special command, which allows you to tie the external graphic file to a particular spot in your document. For example, you might use

```
\begin{figure}[htbp]
        \special{...}  %%-- tie to graphics file
        \caption{...}\label{...}
\end{figure}
```

The argument of the \special command contains the external file's name and possibly information about how the graphic is to be printed (for example, rotated or rescaled). LaTeX makes no attempt to understand the information provided by the \special command, but simply includes its name and printing options into the resulting .DVI file. It is up to the device driver that takes the .DVI file and creates the screen display or printed output to integrate correctly the graphic file.

Many DVI device drivers are available, but only a few know how to include graphic files. If you adopt this approach for placing pictures in your documents, you must use special implementations of LaTeX (at least for the screen and printer device drivers) and your document thus ceases to be portable. Nevertheless, this is the only way for making complex graphics an integral part of your document. Using graphic files in the PCL or PostScript format, you can even include half-tone photographs in your document. Section 6.5 provides details and examples of including PCL and PostScript graphic files.

6.2   The Picture Environment

With LaTeX's picture environment, simple graphs and pictures can be created. The following graphic is produced by the commands to the right.

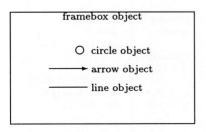

```
\setlength{\unitlength}{0.04in}
\begin{picture}(50,30)(0,0)
   \put(0,0){\framebox(50,30)[t]
             {framebox object}}
   \put(10,10){\line(1,0){10}}
   \put(21,9){line object}
   \put(10,15){\vector(1,0){10}}
   \put(21,14){arrow object}
   \put(18,20){\circle{2}}
   \put(21,19){circle object}
\end{picture}
```

Before any `picture` is begun, the length of a "plotting unit" must be set with the command `\setlength{\unitlength}{xx}` where `xx` is the physical length of one plotting unit (the default is one point = 1/72 of an inch). All (x, y) coordinates and lengths are specified as multiples of the plotting unit length; thus the `unitlength` should be fairly small to get sufficient resolution. A standard x-y coordinate system is used to define the location of all objects in the picture.

The `\begin{picture}(xwidth,ywidth)(xlowleft,ylowleft)` statement defines the beginning of the picture, the width and height of the picture, and the coordinates of the lower-left corner, all in plotting units. To center a picture, enclose the picture environment in `\begin{center}` ... `\end{center}`.

6.2.1   Summary of Picture Commands

Once the picture environment is entered, objects are placed in the plotting area with the command

$$\text{\texttt{\textbackslash put\{xanchor,yanchor\}\{}}\textit{picture object + parameters}\text{\texttt{\}}}$$

The `{xanchor,yanchor}` are the "anchor" coordinates of the object which, usually specify the (lower) left corner (although it is the center for circles and ovals). The parameters of the object then define the size and orientation of the object.

The objects supported by LaTeX are `\line` (a line), `\vector` (an arrow), `\circle` (a circle), `\oval` (an oval or part of one), `\bezier` (a bezier quadratic spline), `\rule` (a filled rectangle), `\framebox` (a hollow rectangle), `\dashbox` (a dashed lined rectangle), and `\shortstack` (a block of text). The use of these picture objects is illustrated by the following examples.

Boxes: `\framebox(`*width,height*`)[`*placement*`]{`*text string*`}`
        `\dashbox{`*dash length*`}(`*width,height*`)[`*placement*`]{`*text string*`}`
        `\makebox(`*width,height*`)[`*placement*`]{`*text string*`}`
        `\rule[`*vertical shift*`]{`*width*`}{`*height*`}`

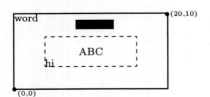

```
\thicklines
\put(0,0){\framebox
        (20,10)[tl]{word}}
\thinlines
\put(4,3){\dashbox
        {.5}(12,4)[bl]{hi}}
\put(8,4){\makebox(4,2){ABC}}
\put(8,8){\rule{.4in}{.1in}}
```

Optional placement arguments are l (left), r (right), t (top), or b (bottom), or any two-letter combination. Omission of a placement argument causes the legend to be centered. A dashed box looks best when the width and height are both multiples of the dash length. Note that \rule is a regular LATEX text-mode command and is not limited to the picture environment. As such, its arguments are actual distances, and not distances expressed in terms of the coordinates of the picture area.

Lines and Arrows: \line(x,y){*xlength*} and \vector(x,y){*xlength*}

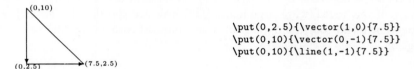

```
\put(0,2.5){\vector(1,0){7.5}}
\put(0,10){\vector(0,-1){7.5}}
\put(0,10){\line(1,-1){7.5}}
```

The coordinate pair x,y *must* be integers and determine the slope ($= y/x$) of the line (or arrow). The x-coordinate of the line changes by x units for every y units change in the y-coordinate. The slope y/x of the line (or arrow) cannot be greater than ±6:1 (or ±4:1). Furthermore, the x and y integers may have no common divisor. As a result, lines and arrows can be drawn with only a finite number of slopes; this is a major limitation of the picture environment. The *xlength* parameter is generally *not* the line length, but rather the change in the x-coordinate from the beginning to the end of the line. However, for vertical and horizontal lines, *xlength* is the true length of the line.

Circles: \circle{*diameter*} and \circle*{*diameter*}

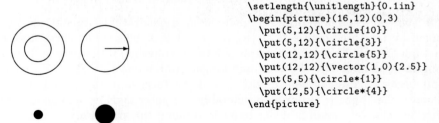

```
\setlength{\unitlength}{0.1in}
\begin{picture}(16,12)(0,3)
   \put(5,12){\circle{10}}
   \put(5,12){\circle{3}}
   \put(12,12){\circle{5}}
   \put(12,12){\vector(1,0){2.5}}
   \put(5,5){\circle*{1}}
   \put(12,5){\circle*{4}}
\end{picture}
```

Notice that \circle* is like \circle except that the circle is filled. LATEX has only a fixed number of different sizes of circles and chooses the one closest to that specified. The largest one here is as big as LATEX can make.

Ovals and Rounded Corners: \oval(*x,y*)[*optional half or quarter argument*]

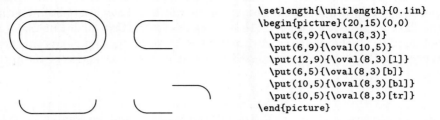

```
\setlength{\unitlength}{0.1in}
\begin{picture}(20,15)(0,0)
   \put(6,9){\oval(8,3)}
   \put(6,9){\oval(10,5)}
   \put(12,9){\oval(8,3)[l]}
   \put(6,5){\oval(8,3)[b]}
   \put(10,5){\oval(8,3)[bl]}
   \put(10,5){\oval(8,3)[tr]}
\end{picture}
```

The center is specified by the \put(x,y) command and the width and height by the *x,y* of the \oval(x,y) argument. Half ovals are specified by l (left), r (right), t (top), or b (bottom), and quarter ovals (rounded corners) by any two-letter combination.

Bezier Curves: \bezier{*n*}(*x₁,y₁*)(*x₂,y₂*)(*x₃,y₃*)

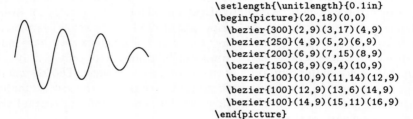

```
\setlength{\unitlength}{0.1in}
\begin{picture}(20,18)(0,0)
   \bezier{300}(2,9)(3,17)(4,9)
   \bezier{250}(4,9)(5,2)(6,9)
   \bezier{200}(6,9)(7,15)(8,9)
   \bezier{150}(8,9)(9,4)(10,9)
   \bezier{100}(10,9)(11,14)(12,9)
   \bezier{100}(12,9)(13,6)(14,9)
   \bezier{100}(14,9)(15,11)(16,9)
\end{picture}
```

Bezier splines can be used in the picture environment only if the style option bezier is selected as one of the document's style options with, for example,

$$\text{\documentstyle[texnotes,bezier,12pt]\{book\}}$$

The \bezier command draws n points along a quadratic (parabolic) curve determined by the three points $P_i \equiv (x_i, y_i)$, $i = 1, 2, 3$. The spline curve does not go through the middle point (unless all points are colinear); rather, the spline curve is tangent to the line $P_2 - P_1$ at P_1 and tangent to the line $P_2 - P_3$ at P_3. Thus multiple bezier splines can be smoothly joined together, as in the preceding example. Beware, the \bezier requires considerably computer memory and should be used only for relatively small graphics to avoid running out of memory.

Text: \put(*x,y*){*text string*}
      \makebox(*width,height*)[*pos.*]{*text string*}
      \frame{*text string*}
      \shortstack[*justification*] {*line 1* \\ *line 2* \\ ... }

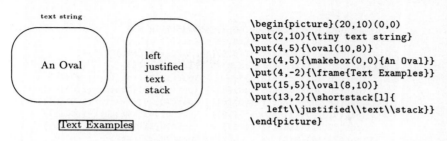

```
\begin{picture}(20,10)(0,0)
\put(2,10){\tiny text string}
\put(4,5){\oval(10,8)}
\put(4,5){\makebox(0,0){An Oval}}
\put(4,-2){\frame{Text Examples}}
\put(15,5){\oval(8,10)}
\put(13,2){\shortstack[l]{
    left\\justified\\text\\stack}}
\end{picture}
```

The x,y coordinates of \put(x,y){\shortstack{...}} and \put(x,y){text} specify the bottom-left position of the text. The \makebox(0,0){...} (a zero size box) centers the text at the x,y anchor points of the \put{x,y}{\makebox..} object. The optional position argument of \makebox can be t,b,l,r,tr,bl, and so on, and causes that position of the caption to be placed at the \put's anchor points. The optional text justification argument of the \shortstack object can be l, c, or r.

Repeating Objects: \multiput$(x,y)(\Delta x, \Delta y)\{n\}\{object\}$

This command puts n copies of *object* in the picture, starting at position (x,y) and incrementing the position by $(\Delta x, \Delta y)$ units each time. For example, the following figure was produced with \multiput(30,0)(2,.5){10}{\circle{.4}}

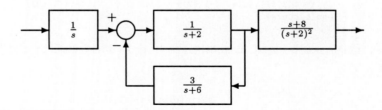

An Example

Although commands for the picture environment are somewhat limited (for example, lines can be drawn only with a limited number of slopes), simple graphics can be generated. Here is an example.

This example was produced by

```
\setlength{\unitlength}{.05in}
\begin{center}
\begin{picture}(80,30)
  \thicklines
```

```
        \put(10,16){\framebox(10,8){$\frac{1}{s}$}}
        \put(32,16){\framebox(16,8){$\frac{1}{s+2}$}}
        \put(54,16){\framebox(16,8){$\frac{s+8}{(s+2)^2}$}}
        \put(32,4){\framebox(16,8){$\frac{3}{s+6}$}}
        \put(26,20){\circle{4}}          \put(4,20){\vector(1,0){6}}
        \put(20,20){\vector(1,0){4}}     \put(28,20){\vector(1,0){4}}
        \put(48,20){\vector(1,0){6}}     \put(70,20){\vector(1,0){6}}
        \put(51,20){\line(0,-1){12}}     \put(51,8){\vector(-1,0){3}}
        \put(32,8){\line(-1,0){6}}       \put(26,8){\vector(0,1){10}}
        \put(23,16){$-$}                 \put(22,22){$+$}
  \end{picture}
  \end{center}
```

6.2.2   Reusing Picture Elements

The \savebox command can be used to create and save a picture for use in other
pictures. The \usebox commands is subsequently used to place this saved picture
in another picture, perhaps multiple times. The syntax of the \savebox command
is

$$\savebox\{\backslash boxname\}(width,height)[placement]\{picture\ definition\}$$

The name of the box (\boxname) in which the picture is to be saved is first defined
with the command \newsavebox{\boxname}. The \savebox works exactly the
same as \makebox, except the output is not printed but rather is saved in \boxname.

For example, suppose a small diamond is needed for several pictures. First,
define a diamond picture and save it in a box called \diamnd with

```
        \setlength{\unitlength}{.1in}
        %--- create and save a diamond image
        \newsavebox{\diamnd}  %-- define the box for saving
        \savebox{\diamnd}(4,4){
            \begin{picture}(4,4)(0,0)
                \put(0,2){\line(1,1){2}}     \put(0,2){\line(1,-1){2}}
                \put(2,4){\line(1,-1){2}}     \put(2,0){\line(1,1){2}}
            \end{picture} }
```

Then this image can be used in another picture, as illustrated by the following
example.

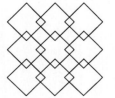

```
        \begin{picture}(10,10)(0,0)
            \multiput(0,0)(3,0){3}{\usebox{\diamnd}}
            \multiput(0,3)(3,0){3}{\usebox{\diamnd}}
            \multiput(0,6)(3,0){3}{\usebox{\diamnd}}
        \end{picture}
        \savebox{\diamnd{}} %--release memory
```

6.3 Extending the `picture` Environment

To augment the limited capabilities of the `picture` environment, special sets of graphics macros have been developed that permit more complex pictures to be created within LaTeX. Two such macro packages are EPIC/EEPIC and PiCTeX. These macro packages define additional graphics commands that permit easy creation of bar graphs and *x-y* graphs and the drawing of ellipses, curves, splines, and lines of various styles and with any slope, as well as many other graphic shapes. These macro packages create figures as part of the LaTeX document; consequently, they can be previewed with your document, a feature not generally enjoyed by other non-LaTeX approaches.

Michael Wichura's PiCTeX macro package is highly recommended. Although, the macros themselves are freely available from many archive sites around the world, the manual (a necessity because of the richness of the command set) is available for about $30 only from TeX Users Group, P.O. Box 869, Santa Barbara, CA 93102-0869.

To use the PiCTeX macros the following statements must be added to the preamble of your document (in the order shown):

```
\input prepicte.tex
\input pictex.pc
\input postpict.tex
```

Then, in the document, you can create a floating centered figure by using the following structure:

```
%%----- PICTEX Template (by. N. Dean Eckhoff)
\begin{figure}[htbp]    %% Begin a floating figure
\centering              %% Used to center the caption.
$$\vbox{                %% Used to center the plot and caption
                        %% in an invisible box.
\beginpicture
   .....                %%%%%%%%%%%%%%%%%%%%%%%%%%%%%%%%%%%%%%
   .....                %%%%%  Use PiCTeX commands to   %%%%%
   .....                %%%%%  construct the lines and  %%%%%
   .....                %%%%%  labels of the figure     %%%%%
   .....                %%%%%%%%%%%%%%%%%%%%%%%%%%%%%%%%%%%%%%
\endpicture}$$
  \parbox{6in}{                    %% Set caption width
  \caption{...}\label{...} }       %% caption & label for figure
\end{figure}
```

There are far too many PiCTeX commands to summarize them here. If you are going to use PiCTeX, there is no substitute for having the manual with all its examples.

Although PiCTeX allows you to create complex figures, it does have its drawbacks. First, many PiCTeX commands are memory intensive, and an `Out of` memory error is frequently encountered when trying to create large or complex figures. Second, while text is in the same font style as used in your document, it can have only the normal horizontal orientation.

6.4   Programs to Generate LaTeX Pictures

Several graphics programs in the public domain allow you to construct technical graphs and figures interactively and will produce a file of LaTeX commands (extended, perhaps, by macro packages such as EEPIC/EPIC or PiCTeX). This file can then be incorporated into in your LaTeX document. Two such widely used programs are GNUPLOT and xfig. GNUPLOT is a program for producing x-y plots of functions and data that provides many options for formatting the graph. This program runs on most computers (VMS, UNIX, AIX, MS-DOS, Amiga-DOS, and others). The xfig is a figure editor that runs under X11. Its point-and-click user interface allows you quickly to create line drawings. In this section, a simple example of using GNUPLOT with LaTeX is given.

6.4.1   A GNUPLOT Example

As an example, the following GNUPLOT commands (issued at the prompt in the GNUPLOT program (in which you find yourself after issuing the command `gnuplot`) produce a LaTeX graphics file called `egplt1.tex`.

```
set terminal latex
set output "gnueg.tex"
set title "This is a plot of $y=\sin(x)$"
set xlabel "This is the $x$ axis"
set ylabel "This is\\the\\$y$ axis"
plot [0:2*pi] [-1.2:1.2] sin(x)
```

The resulting output file can then be inserted into your LaTeX document as, for example, a floating figure (see Fig. 6.1) by using

```
\begin{figure}[htb]
   \centering
      \input{gnueg}
   \vspace{-.3in}
   \caption{A simple graph produced with
     {\sf GNUPLOT} example.}\label{egplt1}
\end{figure}
```

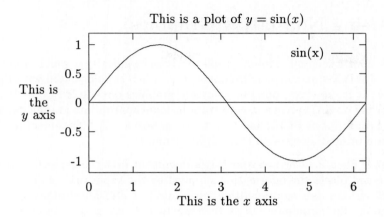

Figure 6.1: A simple GNUPLOT example.

Rather than have GNUPLOT immediately plot to a LATEX file, as just indicated, you can first use the GNUPLOT `set` and `replot` commands to redraw the graph on the screen until the graph is composed as desired (that is, you construct the graph piece by piece). Once the graph is displayed properly on the screen, use the following commands to generate the `egplt1.tex` file.

```
set terminal latex
set output "egplt1.tex"
replot
```

GNUPLOT has a rich set of commands for composing a graph; these are discussed in the GNUPLOT Manual (distributed with the program). One major deficiency with the resulting plots in LATEX is the restriction that all captions and axis labels must be horizontal (no vertically oriented text can be printed).

GNUPLOT can produce very complex plots. It can plot functions and data from external data files, use different line and symbol types, draw error bars on data points, and create plots of different size and shape, and it allows great flexibility in labeling and placing captions. Moreover, LATEX picture files produced by GNUPLOT are simple ASCII files which can be edited to make minor changes in titles, font faces, and the like. This manual editing is often easier than going back to GNUPLOT and modifying the plot.

The GNUPLOT command `save` causes all the commands used to create the current graph to be saved to a file. The `load` command then retrieves these commands from the file so that you can refine the graph at some later time. GNUPLOT can also output the graph to a file in PostScript or HPGL format.

6.5   Using Non-LaTeX Graphics

Technical reports generally require graphics whose complexity is well beyond the capabilities of LaTeX's `picture` environment, even when supplemented with PiCTeX's extensions. It is, however, possible to create graphics outside LaTeX with your favorite drawing or CAD program, save them in some appropriate graphic format (for example, PostScript or PCL), and then tie them into a LaTeX document so that the graphics are printed along with the LaTeX document.

A graphic file is attached to your LaTeX document with the `\special` command. This command places the information supplied by the `\special` command (the file name, and perhaps its size, orientation, etc.) into the .DVI file without any attempt to process the file's contents. It is then up to the screen or printer driver that subsequently processes the .DVI file to correctly interpret the graphic file and to send the right commands to the screen or printer to draw the graphics.

Few DVI printer drivers and fewer screen drivers know how to process graphics files specified by the `\special` commands. Most just leave a blank in the output. Some, however, can correctly interpret files written in special graphic languages (for example, PostScript, PCL, BMP, PCX, MSP, and several others). You must find a DVI driver that can process the form of graphic files that you want to use.

One of the most widely used (LaTeX)TeX implementations for DOS microcomputers is the freely available emTeX package. This package comes with DVI printer drivers for about fifteen different types of printers. Moreover, these drivers allow the importation of MSP (Microsoft Paint), PCX (PC Paintbrush), and BMP (PM Bitmap) raster graphic files. A graphic file in one of these formats is inserted into the document with the command `\special{em:graph` *filespec*`}` where *filspec* is the graphic file name.

In addition to DVI printer/screen drivers that come with a particular implementation of (LaTeX)TeX, there are many other stand-alone drivers available. Some are commercial products, but many are freely available through the Internet. In this section, the use of two particular DVI printer drivers is discussed. The first is representative of drivers that can import raster (bit-mapped) graphic files. The second, and much more powerful driver, allows the use of PostScript graphic files, which because of their vector graphic nature, can be modified (for example, resized) before the graphic is printed.

6.5.1   Importing PCL Graphics Files

A PCL graphics file can be inserted into a LaTeX document provided (1) a printer is used that can understand this type of file (for example, an HP LaserJet printer),

and (2) your DVI printer driver knows how to interpret a `.PCL` file specified by the
`\special` command. One such printer driver is PTIHP a product of Personal TEX,
Inc., 12 Madrona Ave., Mill Valley, CA 94941, USA. Most other DVI drivers that
can import other types of bit-mapped graphic files are used in the same way as
described in this section for PTIHP.

Here is an example graphic.

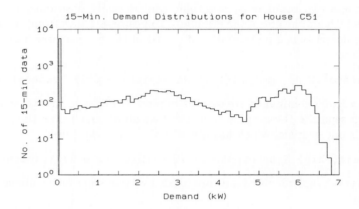

This graphic was inserted with the command

> `\vspace{2.2in} \hspace*{0.6in} \special{pcl:fdemand.pcl}`

The key to inserting a graphic is to first position LATEX on the page where you
want the lower-left corner of the graphic to be placed. To do this you must know
the width and height of the PCL graphic. This is the reason for the `\vspace` and
`\hspace` commands in this example.

Inserting a graphic into a document with the `\special` has one major disadvantage. The graphic usually will not be displayed when previewing the DVI file since
most DVI screen drivers do not know how to interpret the `\special` information.
A blank space will be inserted on the screen. However, the graphic will be printed
correctly (provided you have positioned it correctly).

Macros for Positioning Graphics

To ease the placement of a PCL graphic, define the two new commands `\setpcl`
and `\centerpcl` by placing

```
\def\setpcl#1#2#3{\vskip#2\relax\noindent\hskip#1\relax%
   \special{pcl:#3}}
\def\centerpcl#1#2#3{\vskip#2\relax\centerline{\hbox to#1%
   {\special{pcl:#3}\hfil}}}
```

into the preamble of your document. Equivalently, you can put these command definitions into a separate file (setpcl.tex say) and use \input setpcl in the preamble, or specify setpcl as a document style option.

With these two commands, a graphic can be easily positioned (provided you know the width and height of the graphic). To position, 1 inch from the left margin, a PCL graphic that is 2 inches tall and stored in the file picture.pcl, you would enter the line

```
\vspace{.2in} \setpcl{1in}{2in}{picture.pcl} \vspace{.2in}
```

The two \vspace commands are needed to place blank space above and below the graphic (to separate the graphic from the text above and below the graphic). To center the same graphic, which has a width of say 4 inches, use

```
\vspace{.2in} \centerpcl{4in}{2in}{picture.pcl} \vspace{.2in}
```

Again the two \vspace commands are needed to give some space above and below the graphic.

With the \setpcl and \centerpcl commands, graphics can be positioned in a variety of ways. Here are some examples showing several ways to position graphics on a page with these commands.

Example 1: A Floating Figure

By using \centerpcl in a figure environment, the imported graphic can be made into a floating object. For example, Fig. 6.2 is a floating figure created by the following sequence.

```
\begin{figure}[htbp]
   \centerpcl{3in}{3in}{friver.pcl}
      \centering
         \parbox{4in}{\caption{Cross-river concentration profiles
         for a point radioisotope release at various positions
         down river from the release point.}\label{riverfig}}
\end{figure}
```

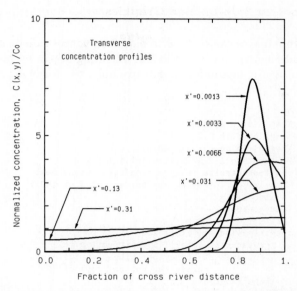

Figure 6.2: Cross-river concentration profiles for a point radioiso-
tope release at various positions down river from the release point.

Example 2: Side-by-Side Graphic and Text

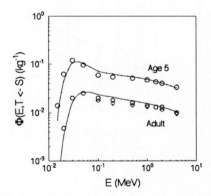

You can also use two `minipages` side by
side to place text beside a figure as in this
example. Here's how it is done.

```
\noindent \begin{minipage}[t]{2.25in}
\setpcl{.25in}{1.75in}{livpan.pcl}
\end{minipage} \hfill
\begin{minipage}[t]{2.6in}
You can also use two \verb|minipages|
side by side to place text beside a
figure as in this example.  Here's how
it is done.
\end{minipage}
```

This same idea can be used to place the caption beside a small figure. You
could put the figure `\caption` command in the right minipage. Additionally, both
minipages could be put between `\begin{figure}` and `\end{figure}` to make the
pair a floating object (see the next example).

Example 3: Floating Side-by-Side Graphics

Two side-by-side minipages can be used to place two figures side by side. Moreover, the two side-by-side figures can be made into a floating object by placing the minipages in the same figure environment. For example, the following input produces Figs. 6.3 and 6.4.

```
\begin{figure}[htbp]
\captionwidth 2.0in
\begin{minipage}[t]{2.40in}
    \centerpcl{2.13in}{1.61in}{leftfig.pcl}
    \footnotesize \hangcaption{Load curtailment
              during the hottest days of 1991}
    \label{figl}
\end{minipage}
\hfill
\begin{minipage}[t]{2.40in}
    \centerpcl{2.13in}{1.61in}{rightfig.pcl}
    \footnotesize \hangcaption{Load curtailment
              during the hottest days of 1992}
    \label{figr}
\end{minipage}
\end{figure}
```

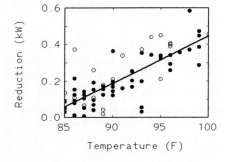

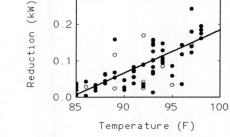

Figure 6.3: Load curtailment during the
hottest days of 1991

Figure 6.4: Load curtailment during the
hottest days of 1992

In Figs. 6.3 and 6.4, a revised `\hangcaption` command (discussed later in Section 8.3) is used rather than the conventional LaTeX `\caption` command. Unlike the `\caption` command, `\hangcaption` will honor the `\footnotesize` command and will also restrict the caption to a width `\captionwidth` that is less than the minipage width.

Putting Graphics into Paragraphs

The preceding examples all placed graphics as floating objects outside any text paragraph. On rare occasion, you might want a graphic to appear in the middle of a paragraph with the lines above and below still right justified. This takes some

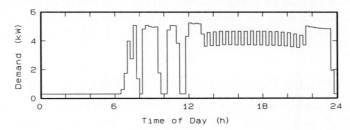

fancy TEX work. For example, the graphic in this paragraph has a height of 1.4 inches and a width of 3.5 inches and the graphic was inserted into this paragraph with the following mystical sequence:

```
... with the lines\vadjust{\vskip 1.4in \centerline{\hbox to
3.50in {\special{pcl:facload.pcl}\hfil}}\vskip .1in} above and...
```

Note in this construct that the graphic will be placed after the line containing the word (here "lines") that is immediately before the placement command sequence (\vadjust...}}}).

By using TEX's box commands and many of its paragraph formatting features, a graphic can be placed almost anywhere in a paragraph. Here is an example in which the graphic is placed in the upper-left corner of the paragraph and the text is made to flow around it. The basic idea is first to define the shape of the paragraph, that is, leave a hole for the graphic. Then the graphic is inserted into a properly sized box and placed in the paragraph's hole. Often it takes considerable "tweaking" to get the dimensions of the hole just right and the graphics placed correctly in the hole. This paragraph was composed even more mystically as follows:

```
{\noindent \global\hangindent=1.75in \global\hangafter=-10
\setbox0\hbox{\special{pcl:abbiefig.pcl}}
\hskip-1.75in\setbox0\hbox to1.70in{\raise-1.5in\box0\hss}%
\dp0=0in\ht0=0in\box0}By using \TeX's box commands...
```

From these two examples, it is seen that the positioning of an external graphic with text flowing around it is very tricky. Fortunately, most scientific graphics will be floating graphics without text on either side, such as Fig. 6.2, and the commands `\setpcl` and `\centerpcl` will suffice. Moreover, when you want to get cute and do fancy positioning of a graphic, it is better to use special macros that have been developed for just such applications, rather than to try to use mystical TeX commands to create space for the graphic in a paragraph. In Chapter 8 two such style packages for positioning graphics (`WRAPFIG` and `PICINPAR`) are demonstrated.

6.5.2   Importing PostScript Graphic Files

If you are fortunate to have access to a PostScript Printer, you can create graphics outside of LaTeX, save them in PostScript format, and import them into your LaTeX document. These "vector" graphic files are generally preferred to "bit-mapped" graphic files (such as `.PCL` files) because they can be easily modified when they are included in your document; the most useful modification is the ability to resize graphics without having to alter the graphics files themselves.

Several DVI PostScript printer drivers permit encapsulated PostScript (`.EPS` or just `.PS` for short) graphics files to be used in LaTeX documents. From Personal TeX, Inc. is the driver PTIPS for DOS microcomputers that incorporates encapsulated PostScript graphic files (`.PS` files) into a document in almost exactly the same way as PTIPCL (see Section 6.5.1) incorporates `.PCL` files. The only difference is that all occurrences of "pcl" in this section are replaced by "ps".

However, by far the most popular and powerful PostScript DVI driver is DVIPS created by Thomas Rokicki. One of the many nice feature about DVIPS is that it is freely available from most TeX archives and can be used on almost any computer platform. This driver, especially when augmented by one of several special macro packages, makes it very easy to print PostScript graphics with your document. In the subsections that follow, a brief introduction on how to use DVIPS and some simple examples are given. But, first, a brief discussion about PostScript files is necessary.

PostScript Files

PostScript graphic files, unlike bit-mapped files, are standard ASCII files that can be edited to modify the graphic or to include some necessary information. This is important since it is sometimes necessary to modify a PostScript file to put it into an acceptable encapsulated PostScript form that can be used in your document.

Encapsulated PostScript is an extension to standard PostScript. In particular, properly encapsulated PostScript files must contain certain comment lines beginning with a double percent symbol %%. The most important one is

%%BoundingBox: x1 y1 x2 y2

in which x1 y1 and x2 y2 are the coordinates of the lower-left and upper-right corners of the figure, respectively, in PostScript units (72 to the inch). If the file has such a statement, then it is probably encapsulated PostScript. Otherwise, you must print the figure, determine its size, and edit in the necessary %%BoundingBox information.

The ability to edit a PostScript file is also useful (provided you know something about the PostScript language) if you want to modify some feature of the graphic without having to recreate the graphic from scratch.

Using DVIPS

If you use DVIPS to convert LᴬTᴇX's output .DVI file into a PostScript file for printing, the \special command is used in the document source file to specify information about the PostScript graphic. With the \special command you can specify .PS file names, scaling information, orientation for the graphic, fonts to be used in the graphic, and many other features. In fact, a complete PostScript picture can be defined inside the argument of the \special command. The 50-page manual that comes with DVIPS explains the many options and capabilities of this fine program. Learning to use all the features available with DVIPS requires considerable effort.

Fortunately, most of us do not need to master the intricacies of DVIPS if all we want to do is include PostScript figures that are created outside LᴬTᴇX. Several style files are freely available that define macros to generate automatically the needed DVIPS \special commands and thus make it easy to incorporate PostScript figures into a document. These macro packages include EPSF, PSFIG, TPIC, METAPOST, and emTeX specials. The use of the first two of these packages is summarized next.

Using EPSF **Macros**

To use the EPSF macros, include the statement \input epsf in the document's preamble, or include its name as a option in the \documentstyle command, for example, \documentstyle[epsf,12pt]{report}. The macro command \epsfbox (or its synonymous command \epsffile) is then used to place a PostScript file graphic into the document. For example, to define a floating figure whose graphic is contained in the file fig1.ps, enter the following.

```
\begin{figure}[htbp]
   \centering \leavemode
   \epsfbox{fig1.ps}
   \caption{....... \label{...}}
\end{figure}
```

Notice the \leavemode statement that is necessary to make the \centering command work properly and produce a figure and caption that are centered horizontally.

If the PostScript file does not have the necessary %%BoundingBox information, it can be provided by \epsfbox's optional argument as, for example,

\epsfbox[0 0 30 50]{fig1.ps}

EPSF also allows a figure to be resized by including, for example, \epsfsizex=3in or \epsfsizey=5cm before the \epsfbox command.

Using PSFIG Macros

The PSFIG macros, written by Trevor Darrell, offer additional figure placement features. In addition to allowing a graphic to be rescaled and providing %%BoundingBox information, this macro set also allows the graphic to be rotated and clipped (that is, only a portion of the graphic is printed). To use PSFIG, put the statement \input psfig in the preamble or add psfig as an option in the \documentstyle command.

Then the \psfig command is used to place a PostScript figure at the current position on the page. The syntax of the \psfig command is

```
\psfig{file=,height=,width=,bbllx=,bblly=,bburx=,bbury=,
       rheight=,rwidth=,angle=,clip=}
```

The various options are explained in the accompanying table. Only those options wanted need be specified. Note, it is important that no spaces appear between the various option arguments.

To creating a floating figure of the graphic in file fig1.ps with the graphic width rescaled to 3.5 inches, rotated counterclockwise by 90 degrees, and clipped to the size specified by the %%BoundingBox statement in the file, use

```
\begin{figure}[htbp]
   \centering \leavemode
   \psfig{file=fig1.ps,width=3.5in,angle=90,clip=}
   \caption{....... \label{...}}
\end{figure}
```

Options for the `\psfig` Command

Command	*Purpose*
`file=`	Following the `=` sign is the file name (including an optional directory path) containing the PostScript graphic. Not an optional item.
`width=`	Desired width of figure.
`height=`	Desired height of figure.
	If both `width` and `height` are omitted, the size is determined by the `BoundingBox` information. If only one size option is specified, the graphic is scaled keeping the original height/width aspect ratio. If both `height` and `width` are specified, the graphic is scaled anamorphically.
`bbllx bblly`	BoundingBox coordinates for the lower-left corner of the graphic.
`bburx bbury`	BoundingBox coordinates for the upper-right corner of the graphic.
`rheight`	The reserved height for the graphic, that is, how high TeX should think the figure is. Defaults to `height`.
`rwidth`	The reserved width for the graphic, that is, how wide TeX should think the figure is. Defaults to `width`.
`clip`	A switch that specifies that no part of the graphic outside the `BoundingBox` is to be printed. No numerical value is provided but the `=` sign must be given.
`angle`	The amount (in degrees) of counterclockwise rotation desired for the printed graphic.

An Example

Here is an example. The left-hand figure is printed in its original size, while the right-hand figure is scaled to a smaller size.

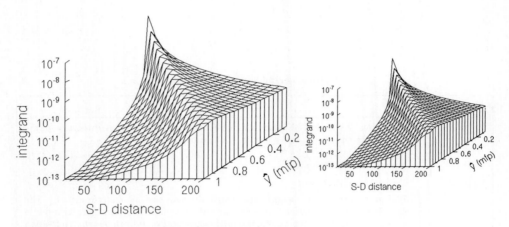

These side-by-side examples were produced with

```
\noindent \begin{minipage}[t]{3.00in}
        \centering \leavemode
        \psfig{file=3dlbrf.ps}
\end{minipage} \hfill
\begin{minipage}[t]{2.00in}
        \centering \leavemode
        \psfig{file=3dlbrf.ps,width=2.0in,height=1.5in}
\end{minipage}
```

Using Non-PostScript Printers with PostScript Graphics

To print a document containing PostScript graphics, a PostScript printer is *not* necessary (although it is the easiest way to print the document). The publicly available program Ghostscript can translate any PostScript file (such as that produced by DVIPS) into a form that can be used by many different types of printers, including non-PostScript LaserJet and dot matrix printers. It can even be used even to preview the PostScript printer file on the computer screen. This program is also available for a great variety of computer platforms, so a LaTeX document with PostScript graphics can easily be ported to different computers even if they do not have PostScript printers. This is a highly recommended utility that at no cost provides PostScript capability to your computer system.

6.6 Producing Graphic Files for LaTeX

The production of a .PS or .PCL file for a LaTeX graphic is often a cumbersome affair. If your graphics program cannot produce this type of graphics file directly, you will have to use a capture program to place in a file the data your drawing program is trying to send to the printer or to the screen. Moreover, you will usually have to convert your graphic file from some other graphic format (such as, PCX, HPGL, TIFF, BMP, or GIF) into the PCL or PS format.

6.6.1 Converting from HPGL Format

Most programs for producing graphs and other technical drawings can output the graphic in the Hewlett-Packard Graphic Language (HPGL). For line drawings this vector graphics language has become a standard, and if you are going to import technical graphics into LaTeX documents, you will frequently have to convert HPGL (also called .PGL) files into .PS or .PCL files. Two programs for performing this format conversion are discussed next.

HP2XX

The freeware program HP2XX, written by Heinz Werntges, is available from many Internet archive sites and is distributed with the source code so that it can be run on almost any computer system. This program can convert .PGL files to both .PS or .PCL files (as well as several other useful formats including PCX, EPIC/LATEX, and emTeX specials formats). This program does the conversion quickly, allows you to specify the size of the converted graphics, and rotate the graphic if necessary, and lets you preview the graphic on the screen to see if you have it right side up.

PRINTGL

The MS-DOS shareware program PRINTGL, written and distributed by Ravitz Software, Inc., (P.O. Box 25068, Lexington, Kentucky 40524-5068), is designed for printing HPGL graphic files on a great variety of printers. More important, it can translate .PGL files into .PS and .PCL files. This program has many translation options such as assigning different line widths to different pens, allowing rotation of the graphic, and changing the graphic's size, to name a few. If you use a MS-DOS microcomputer, this is an excellent program to have.

6.6.2 More General Graphic Conversion Programs

Besides the specialized programs discussed for converting .PGL graphic files, many other programs can convert a graphic file from one format to another. A commercial MS-DOS/Windows program that the author has found useful is HiJack (Inset Systems, 71 Commerce Drive, Brookfield, CT 06804), which can convert among over 30 different graphics file formats.

Also, a freeware collection of file conversion programs called PBMPLUS can be found in many Internet archives. This collection of program source codes can be compiled for many computer systems. In this code package, there are specific programs to convert between many different graphics formats, including the ability to convert most types of graphic files to PostScript format.

6.6.3 Creating PostScript Graphics with PSTricks

Timothy Van Zandt has created a set of PostScript-based (LA)TEX macros that allow you to create complex pictures for your LATEX documents. This collection of macros, known as PSTricks, is freely available from most TEX archives on the Internet. With the tools provided by PSTricks, you can create pictures with all sorts of special effects such as color, rotation, overlays, and shadings. Graphics can be composed with a variety of curves, lines, plots, trees, grids, polygons and many other graphic objects. Text and graphic objects can be scaled rotated, and even distorted. PSTricks also has many macros for connecting information or nodes which are useful for making trees and graphs, mathematical diagrams, linguistic diagrams, and connecting ideas visually. If you need to include many special graphics effects into a document and you have a PostScript printer, then PSTricks is highly recommended.

Chapter 7

Large Documents

7.1   The Root File

When preparing large reports, theses, papers, and the like, it is easier to work on them by chapters or sections. The way to do this is to create a separate .TEX file for each chapters or section and a "root" .TEX file that (1) specifies the type of document, (2) the style and formatting to be used, (3) any new commands or macros you will be using, (4) commands to create special parts (for example, a table of contents or an index), and (5) the particular .TEX files to be included. In Fig. 7.1 an example of a root file is given that you LaTeX consisting of several .TEX files.

The root file has two parts: first is the *preamble* where information about styles, page dimensions, and new or redefined commands (macros) are placed. The second portion between the \begin{document} and \end{document} contains the names of the .TEX files containing the document text as well as other commands to generate special sections, such as the table of contents.

Note the two \includeonly statements in Fig. 7.1, one of which is commented out (with the % symbol). The uncommented statement is used to work on only a single part of the document (here ch2.tex). When the whole document is to be processed, switch the % between these two \includeonly statements. Also uncomment the lines containing tableofcontents and listoffigures when ready to produce the final document.

```
%==================== EXAMPLE ROOT FILE ====================
\documentstyle[texnotes,mymacros,12pt]{report}
%===================================== PREAMBLE
%---------- Input other macro files
\input table
\input setpcl

%---------- Command redefinitions and new commands
\newcommand{\be}{\begin{equation}}
\newcommand{\ee}{\end{equation}}
\renewcommand{\bigskip}{\vspace{.2in}}

%---------- Modify dimensions of page elements
\oddsidemargin .25in    \evensidemargin .25in  \textwidth 6in
\topmargin     -.40in   \headheight     .3in   \headsep   .4in
\textheight    8.4in    \footheight     .2in   \footskip .7in
\parskip       1.5ex

%---------- Misc. preamble material
\font\incha=cminch    %-- inch high font
\hyphenation{brems-strahl-ung}
\def\footmsg{\LaTeX\ Notes}

%---------- Files to be included this run
%\includeonly{cover,ch1,ch2,ch3,ch4,biblio,app}  %everything
\includeonly{ch2}                                %part of document

%=================================== ALL FILES IN DOCUMENT
\begin{document}
   \include{cover}
%  \pagenumbering{roman} \setcounter{page}{0} \tableofcontents
%  \listoffigures
   \include{ch1}
   \include{ch2}
   \include{ch3}
   \include{ch4}
   \include{biblio}
   \include{app}
\end{document}
%==========================================================
```

Figure 7.1: Example root file for a large document

7.2 Macros in the Preamble

In the preamble of the root file, you can include definitions of new commands and environments, as well as new definitions for existing commands. The ability to create such new commands and environments is the hallmark of a LaTeXpert. A good LaTeX document should have few complex series of nested commands in the document proper. Rather, new commands and environments should be created so that the writer can concentrate on what he or she is writing and not be distracted by wrestling with formatting problems during the writing phase.

In Chapter 9, methods for creating macros together with several useful examples are presented. Here are a few simple examples to show how macros are placed in the preamble.

```
%------------------- New Commands
\newcommand{\be}{\begin{equation}}    %-- start no. equation mode
\newcommand{\ee}{\end{equation}}      %-- end no. equation mode
\newcommand{\br}{\mbox{\bf r}}        %-- bold r for eqs. in math
\newcommand{\bO}{{\bf \Omega}}        %-- bold cap Omega for math
\newcommand{\bhd}[1]{\noindent {\bf #1}}    %-- bold heading

%------------------- Redefine Old Commands
\renewcommand{\bigskip}{\vspace{.5in}} %-- give bigger \bigskip
\makeatletter  %-- change width for page number in TOC
   \renewcommand{\@pnumwidth}{2.4em}
\makeatother

%------------------- New Environments
\newenvironment{reflist}{\begin{list}{}{\listparindent -.25in
        \topsep .25in } \item \  \vspace{-.45in} }{\end{list}}

%------------------- Bring in Macro Files
\input tables          %-- macros for creating complex tables
\input newmacros        %-- new useful macros
\input epsf            %-- macros for positioning PS files
```

Over time you will acquire many useful macros that you will want available for all your documents. Rather than place them individually in the preamble, put them in a separate file (with extension .TEX) and bring them into a document with the \input command as illustrated in the above example. Equivalently, you can place them in a style (.STY) file and include this style file as a style option in the \documentstyle command (see Fig. 7.1).

Also notice that preamble macros that involve TEX and LATEX internal variables (those with @ as part of their names) must be placed between the statements \makeatletter and \makeatother. When placed in style files (.STY), these bracketing statements are not necessary.

7.3   Loading Style Files

Style files are a special type of macro file. However, they are generally involved with making changes at the heart of LATEX or even of TEX. As such, they alter commands that include the @ symbol. For example, a style file might include the statement \def\rightmark{\expandafter\@rightmark\botmark} Files that contain such statements should be read into a document through the optional style parameter list in the \documentstyle command as, for example,

\documentstyle[texnotes,mystyle,12pt]{report}.

In this example texnotes and mystyle are style files (with extension .STY) to be included in the document. Note that the order of listing the style files determines which commands are entered first.

Sometimes you will want to have a style file loaded after all other style files and preamble commands have been entered. It is possible, but unusual, to load style files and commands containing the @ symbol from within the preamble by bracketing them with \makeatletter and \makeatother, as in

```
\makeatletter
    \def\rightmark{\expandafter\@rightmark\botmark}
    \input wrapfig.sty
\makeatother
```

Finally, be aware of the danger of using too many style files together. One file can redefine parameters or commands set by another. This can cause great havoc in your document. Sometimes the problem can be cured by entering the style files in a different order. Also, trying to load too many style files may exhaust the internal memory of your TEX compiler.

7.4   Front Matter

Before the chapters of your report or book, there generally will be several pages of front matter: title page, dedication, preface, list of contents, list of figures, list of tables, and so on.

7.4.1 Title Page

For the title page, it is often easier to lay out a page using \vspace, \Huge, and other such standard commands, and to avoid any of the \title, \author, and other special commands that are used by LATEX to create title pages. Although this approach is contrary to the LATEX philosophy of freeing the user from formatting concerns, it does allow you to create your own cover design. For example, the cover page of an early draft of this book was produced with

```
\vspace*{1in} \thispagestyle{empty}
\begin{centering}
   \rule{6in}{.04in}\\                     \vspace{.25in}
   {\incha LATEX\\ \vspace{.4in} NOTES}\\  \vspace{.1in}
   \rule{6in}{.04in}\\                     \vspace{.5in}
   \Huge    Version 1.3\\                  \vspace{.75in}
   \large   compiled by\\                  \vspace{.3in}
   \LARGE   {\bf J. Kenneth Shultis} \\    \vspace{.3in}
   \large   Dept. of Nuclear Engineering \\
            Kansas State University\\
            Manhattan, KS 66506 \\
\end{centering}
```

If you are using a prescribe journal style (for example, REVTEX.STY or IEEE.STY, then, of course, you should use the style's title-page commands to create the title page and not perform your own formatting.

7.4.2 Preface

Create the preface like any other chapter using the \chapter*{Preface} command, where the * prevents any incrementing of the chapter counter and suppresses any numbering or entries in the table of contents.

7.4.3 Table of Contents

The \tableofcontents command in the root file shown in Fig. 7.1 will automatically cause a table of contents to be generated. Actually this command causes a file called fn.TOC (where fn is the name of the root file) to be created, and the file by the same name created in the *previous* run is used in creating the index in the .DVI file. Thus it takes at least two runs to create a table of contents that reflects the current pagination and sectioning of the document. If the pagination of your table of contents affects the pagination of the remainder of the document, then *three* passes are necessary. On the second pass, the number of pages in the table of contents may change, thereby changing the page numbering in the rest of document. Only if the pagination of the front matter is independent of the pagination of the main document (as in this document) will two passes suffice.

This multiple-pass procedure for creating a table of contents allows you to edit and modify the `fn.TOC` file prior to LaTeXing the whole document for the last time. In this way you can cause the table of contents to be printed as you want.

The amount of detail included in the table of contents is controlled by the counter `tocdepth`. The value of this counter determines the level of the least significant sectional unit to be included. Chapters are level 0, sections are level 1, subsections level 2, and so on. Thus, to include only chapters and sections titles in the table of contents, place in the preamble `\setcounter{tocdepth}{1}`.

7.4.4   Lists of Figures and Tables

LaTeX will automatically produce a list of figures with their captions if the command `\listoffigures` is encountered during the processing of the root file. Similarly, a `\listoftables` command will produce a list of figures and their captions. The page numbers used in these lists are those found during the previous processing of the file. Thus, to ensure correct pagination, the root file has to be processed at least twice.

Often the captions used in tables and figures are very lengthy, and an abbreviated caption for the list of tables and figures is desired. You may manually edit the `.LOF` and `.LOT` files created during the first processing. However, a better way is to provide the figure or table with a shorter caption to be used in the lists. The general form of the `\caption` command is

$$\texttt{\textbackslash caption[}\textit{entry-for-LOF/LOT}\texttt{]\{}\textit{caption-for-figure/table}\texttt{\}}$$

7.4.5   Adding Entries to Contents, Tables, and Figures Lists

If you use the ∗ form of sectioning commands to produce an unnumbered heading, no entry will be made to the table of contents `.TOC` file. However, you can manually add an entry for such a section or for any other item you want included. To add an entry, denoted by *entry*, to either the `.TOC` `.LOF` or `.LOT` file, use the command

$$\texttt{\textbackslash addcontentsline\{}\textit{file}\texttt{\}\{}\textit{format}\texttt{\}\{}\textit{entry}\texttt{\}}$$

Here *file* is the file to which *entry* is to be added (either `TOC`, `LOF`, or `LOT`). The *format* parameter controls the format of the entry and must be `figure` or `table` if *file* is LOF or LOT, respectively. If *file* is TOC, then *format* is the appropriate sectional unit such as chapter or subsection.

To add a section number to the table of contents entry and to make the entry align with the other subsection entries, use

```
\addcontentsline{toc}{subsection}{\protect%
                    \numberline{5.3.7}{Test Title}}
```

7.4.6 Roman Page Numbering for Front Matter

Pagination style and numbering for the front matter will generally be different (usually lowercase roman numerals) from that of the rest of the document (usually arabic numbers beginning with 1 on the first page of Chapter 1). This change in pagination between the front matter and the body of the document is easily done in LaTeX. First place the command \pagenumbering{roman} before the first part of the front matter (for example, in Fig. 7.1 before the \tableofcontents statement). Then on the first page of the document body (usually right after the first \chapter{...} command in the body) put the command \pagenumbering{arabic}.

7.4.7 Reformatting the Table of Contents

The spacing between entries in the table of contents (or lists of figures and tables) is controlled by the parameter \parskip. You may want extra space between paragraphs in the document (also controlled by \parskip) and yet not between the entries in the table of contents. To force the table of contents to be single spaced while placing separation between text paragraphs, the \tableofcontents line in the root file should resemble

```
\parskip 0ex \tableofcontents   \parskip 1.5ex
```

In the table of contents, LaTeX places a row of dots between a heading entry on the left and its page numbers on the right. The spacing between these dots is controlled by the parameter @dotsep. To eliminate the dots altogether, set the spacing between dots (in math units, where 18 mu = 1 em) to be so large that the first dot will not appear on the page. To do this, place the following in the preamble.

```
\makeatletter
   \renewcommand{\@dotsep}{500}   %-- turn off TOC dots
\makeatother
```

Also, you will find that, if you have many pages (> 999) or if your use a long page numbering scheme (for example, *section-page*), the box used for the page numbers in the table of contents will be too small, and the leader dots will overlap the page numbers. To avoid this, change the box width for the page numbers by placing in the preamble something like

```
\makeatletter
    \renewcommand{\@pnumwidth}{2.4em}   %-- TOC Page No. width
\makeatother
```

7.5   Excluding Part of the Input

When working on a long .TEX file, it is convenient to exclude parts of the file from being LATEXed so as to speed the processing time. Perhaps the simplest way is to put \iffalse at the beginning of the text to be ignored and \fi at the end of the excluded text.

7.6   Footnotes

Footnotes are readily added to a LATEX document with the \footnote[*num*]{*text*} command. Here *num* is an optional number for the footnote. If it is omitted, the next footnote number will automatically be used.

Here is a footnote example in a minipage environment[a] where letters are normally used rather than numbers for footnote symbols.

---
   [a]Normally, the footnote command cannot be used in a "box" environment. The minipage is an exception.

```
Here is a footnote example in a
minipage environment\footnote{%
Normally, the \verb|footnote|
command cannot be used in a
``box" environment. The minipage
is an exception.} where letters
are normally used rather than
numbers for footnote symbols.
```

Footnotes are sequentially numbered throughout a chapter. The counter for footnotes is automatically reset to 1 at the beginning of each new chapter. Long footnotes can be broken across a page boundary by LATEX.

7.6.1   Footnotes in a Heading[1]

The \footnote command is fragile and must be protected when attached to a moving argument such as a section heading (that is, use \protect\footnote{...}).

---
[1]This is a footnote referenced in a subsection heading

An alternative way to place a footnote reference in a section heading is to use the optional argument in the \section command so that \footnote is no longer in a "moving argument" and hence no longer needs to be protected. For example the heading for this subsection was produced with

```
\section[Footnotes in a Heading]{Footnotes in a Heading\footnote{This is a
        footnote referenced in a subsection heading}}
```

7.6.2 Changing the Footnote Symbol

The footnote symbols ∗ † ‡ § ¶ ‖ ∗∗ †† ‡‡ can be used instead of numbers by placing the following command in the preamble (or body) of your document.

```
\renewcommand{\thefootnote}{\fnsymbol{footnote}}
```

Since there are only nine footnote symbols, make sure that no chapter has more that nine footnotes.

To specify a particular footnote symbol, the optional argument of the \footnote command is used, for example, \footnote[2]{...}. The footnote symbols can be restored to the normal arabic form with

```
\renewcommand{\thefootnote}{\arabic{footnote}}
```

7.6.3 Footnotes inside Boxes

The \footnote command can be used only in normal paragraph mode. To attach a footnote to text that is in a box, use the pair of commands \footnotemark[*num*] and \footnotetext[*num*]{*text*}, as in the following example.

Footnotes attached to text in a box[b] must be treated differently than footnotes in normal text.

---
[b]This is a word in a framebox.

```
Footnotes attached to \fbox{%
text in a box\footnotemark}
must be treated differently
than footnotes in normal text.
\footnotetext[2]{This is a word
in a framebox.}
```

7.7 Cross References

One of the great powers of LaTeX is the ability to refer to some document part that has a number (for example, a chapter, section, subsection, equation, etc.) anywhere in the document without having to keep track of the numbering.

To make forward or backward references to chapters, sections, tables, figures, equations, `eqnarrays`, and items in an `enumerate` environment use the `\label` command to attach a reference *key* to the item. This `\label` command is used to define the reference key immediately after the item to which you may want to make a reference. For example, if a reference is to be made elsewhere in the document to a specific chapter, then, when that chapter is defined, you might input

```
\chapter{An Important Chapter}\label{imptchpt}
```

Here the reference key to this chapter is `imptchpt`. Whenever you want to refer to this chapter, use `\ref{imptchpt}`, and whenever you want to refer to the page on which this chapter begins use `\pageref{imptchpt}`. For example, you might enter

```
The most important theorems are discussed in
Chapter~\ref{imptchpt}, which begins on page~\pageref{imptchpt}.
```

7.8   Citations and Bibliography

A nice feature of LaTeX [2, 3] is its ability to make citations and their numbering relatively easy. In preparing a large document, it is usual to add and delete references during the many revisions, and LaTeX makes this job relatively easy.

7.8.1   The Bibliography List

The trick to referencing in LaTeX is first to make an itemized bibliography list and then to include it in the `.TEX` file (usually at the end) enclosed by the environment command `\begin{thebibliography}{`*size*`...\end{thebibliography}` where *size* is the largest (widest) anticipated citation number (which is used to determine the spacing needed in the bibliographic list). For example, if 3-digit citation numbers are anticipated, then set *size* = 999. In the bibliography list, each reference is identified with the `\bibitem{`*key*`}`, where *key* is some unique identifier for the reference that follows. Then, in the text you need only use `\cite{`*key*`}` to have the citation inserted. A typical bibliography list might look like

```
\begin{thebibliography}{9}
    \bibitem{La86} L. Lamport, \LaTeX:
        {\it A Document Preparation System},
        Addison-Wesley, New York, NY 1986.
    \bibitem{CSF} A. B. Chilton, J. K. Shultis
        and R. E. Faw,
        {\it Principles of Radiation Shielding},
        Prentice-Hall, New York, NY 1984.
\end{thebibliography}
```

7.8.2   Making References in the Text

Once the bibliography file is created, you can easily reference your favorite books [2, 1] or even your favorite page [1, page 193]. This output is produced with

```
Once the bibliography file is created, you can easily reference
your favorite books \cite{La86,CSF} or even your favorite page
\cite[page 193]{CSF}.  This output is produced with
```

A word of warning. LATEX numbers the references in the order that they appear in the bibliography list *not* in the order of their citation in the text. You need to reorder manually your bibliography list if you seek ascending reference numbering throughout the document.

7.8.3   Printing the Bibliography

LATEX automatically begins printing the bibliography on a new page when it encounters the bibliography list in the input file. No special commands are needed! See the example bibliography output at the end of this chapter. In **article** document style the bibliography is entitled "References" whereas in **book** and **report** styles it is labeled "Bibliography".

7.8.4   Citation Variations

Instead of using numbers inside square brackets for references, LATEX lets you use any symbolism you want. For example, the last item in the bibliography list used in this chapter is

```
\bibitem[NONAME]{junk} N. O. Name, {\it Never Referenced
       Book}, NoName Publ. Co., NoWhere U.S.A., 1991.
```

where [NONAME] is the citation label to be used in place of citation numbers. Then, to make this citation [NONAME, page 0], you would enter:

```
... make this citation \cite[page 0]{junk}, you would ...
```

7.9   References and Citations in Captions

The \caption command used in figures and tables is fragile. This means that other commands cannot be embedded in the caption without first protecting them. Here is an example of a table whose captions contains both a citation and a reference to a table.

Table 7.1: Test table whose caption contains a reference, in this case to itself, Table 7.1, and has a citation [2] to a bibliographic item

Number of References and Citations												
3	4	7	5	7	3	5	7	11	8	4	5	7
7	8	0	5	8	4	6	7	5	13	1	2	7
3	1	1	5	2	0	1	8	4	7	3	0	1

The caption for this table was produced with the following input statements. Notice that both the \ref and \cite commands in the caption must be protected.

```
\caption{Test table whose caption contains a reference,
         in this case to itself, Table~\protect\ref{reftable},
         and has a citation \protect\cite{La86} to a bibliographic
         item} \label{reftable}
```

The same trick will not work for making a footnote reference in the caption of a table. Using \protect\footnote produces *two* footnotes! One awkward way to put a footnote reference into the table caption is to manually place the symbol in the caption and also to manually place the footnote after the table.

7.10   Making an Index

Generating an index for a large document is a complex affair. LATEX helps automate the process, but it still involves a lot of manual work. Here is the procedure.

Step 1: Use the \index command throughout your document next to the each word where an index entry should be made, for example,

```
...used violins, tubas, and bagpipes\index{instruments} in the...
```

When ready to start making the index, place the command \makeindex in the preamble of the root file. The \index command in the input files is normally ignored by LATEX. The \makeindex command, however, causes LATEX to process the \index entries and create an .IDX file (with the same name as that of the root document) that contains an entry for each \index item. The entries in the .IDX file look something like

```
        ...
\indexentry{instruments}{59}
\indexentry{apples}{62}
\indexentry{bad apples}{63}
        ...
```

Generally, you will not use the \makeindex command until you have a final version of the document and are ready to do the final printing.

Step 2: The next step is performed outside LaTeX. With your editor take the .IDX file and (1) alphabetize the entries, (2) combine similar entries, (3) create second- and third-level entries, and (4) reformat to obtain a file of the form

```
    ...
\item instruments 63, 75, 127
    \subitem bagpipes, 63
        \subsubitem sound of, 75, 89
\item ions 5, 25, 67, 122
\indexspace
\item jack-o'-lantern 52
\item jargon 1, 15, 273
    ...
```

The \indexspace forces a separation between the i and j entries in the index that will eventually be produced. Also you can add to the basic form shown. For example, you could have all primary entries in boldface by using {\bf instruments}, for example, in the preceding file.

Step 3: At the place in your document where you want the index to be printed (usually at the end), put the lines created in step 2 between \begin{theindex}... \end{theindex}. When LaTeX encounters this entry, it will begin a new page, place a large index title, and produce a two-column index.

7.10.1 Doing It Yourself

The above procedure is cumbersome at best. Often it is easier while proofreading the final draft to directly create with your editor the file generated in Step 2 above. Alternatively, several programs are available that will more easily prepare an index file (after manually entering the various entries) whose output you can convert into the form needed by step 2. These manually produced index files can then be printed by LaTeX using the method of step 3.

7.10.2   The MAKEINDEX Program

A freely available program MAKEINDEX will greatly automate the creation of an index. This C program was written by Pehong Chen assisted by M. Harrison and Leslie Lamport, and it can be found in many Internet TEX archives.

Creating an index with this program also involves several steps but requires far less manual effort. Here is the procedure.

1. Mark each word(s) for which you want an entry in the index (with special notation used for subentries and cross references), specify the `makeidx` option in the `\documentstyle` command, place the `\makeindex` command in the preamble, and just before the `\end{document}` place the commands

   `\cleardoublepage` `\printindex`

2. After compiling your document file (for example, `MYDOC.TEX`) for the first time, an `.IDX` file will be produced (for example, `MYDOC.IDX`).

3. Then run the MAKEINDEX program to create an index file (`MYDOC.IND`) with the command `MAKEIDX MYDOC.IDX`.

4. Finally, LaTeX your document file one more time to produced a finished index at the end of your document.

Bibliography

[1] A. B. Chilton, J. K. Shultis and R. E. Faw, *Principles of Radiation Shielding*, Prentice Hall, New York, NY, 1984.

[2] L. Lamport, LATEX: *A Document Preparation System*, Addison-Wesley, New York, NY, 1986.

[3] J. Hahn, *LATEX for Everyone*, Personal TEX, Inc., Mill Valley, CA, 1991.

[4] D. L. Knuth, *The TeXbook*, Addison-Wesley, New York, NY, 1990.

[5] A. Johnstone, *LATEX Concisely*, Prentice Hall, New York, NY, 1992.

[NONAME] N. O. Name, *Never Referenced Book*, NoName Publ. Co., NoWhere, U.S.A., 1991.

This was produced from the bibliography list

```
\begin{thebibliography}{NONAME}
\thispagestyle{texnotes}
\bibitem{CSF}  A. B. Chilton, J. K. Shultis and R. E. Faw,
               {\it Principles of Radiation Shielding},
               Prentice Hall, New York, NY, 1984.
\bibitem{La86} L. Lamport, \LaTeX: {\it A Document Preparation
               System}, Addison-Wesley, New York, NY, 1986.
\bibitem{Ha91} J. Hahn, {\it \LaTeX for Everyone}, Personal
               \TeX, Inc., Mill Valley, CA, 1991.
\bibitem{Kn90} D. L. Knuth, (\it The TeXbook}, Addison-Wesley,
               New York, NY, 1990.
\bibitem{Jo92} A. Johnstone, {\it \LaTeX\ Concisely},
               Prentice Hall, New York, NY, 1992.
\bibitem[NONAME]{junk} N. O. Name, {\it Never Referenced Book},
               NoName Publ. Co., NoWhere, U.S.A., 1991.
\end{thebibliography}
```

Chapter 8

Useful Styles

One great feature of LaTeX is its ability to use style (.STY) files to change formatting features of the document or to extend the capabilities of LaTeX. Most extensions to LaTeX require more than the few lines of macro code that have been used in most of the examples in the previous chapters, and it generally takes considerable effort and (LA)TeX skill to develop a new style file or macro set. Fortunately, the (LA)TeX community is a sharing one, and collections of a great number of style files can be found in many Internet archives. Once you learn how to use the Internet to obtain style files from TeX archives, you will have gained the ability to take LaTeX far beyond its original capabilities.

In this chapter, a few style files are that are particularly useful or interesting are presented, primarily to illustrate the wide variety of formatting that can be achieved. But before showing these example styles, a brief word is appropriate about finding the style file that is most suitable for a particular application.

8.1   Finding and Obtaining Style Files

If you have a special formatting problem, chances are that someone has already written a style file that will take care of it and has contributed it to the growing collection of freely available styles macros. But how to find it? David Jones has, for the past few years, maintained an annotated summary of the many style files available from Internet archives. This summary can be obtained via anonymous ftp from `theory.lcs.mit.edu` in directory `./pub/tex/TeX-index`. The file `TeX-index` may also be found in other Internet archives (see the following Section).

8.1.1 Where to Find Style Files

Once you have determined the name of a style file that appears useful, you must obtain it from an archive site. Several sites around the world support the CTAN (Comprehensive TeX Archive Network). Each CTAN site has identical material and maintains authoritative copies of the many files. By far the best way to get files from these sites is via the Internet and to use anonymous ftp to download the desired file.

Some CTAN sites are `ftp.uni-stuttgart.de` [128.69.1.12] with TeX root directory `.soft/tex`; `ftp.tex.ac.uk` [134.151.44.19], root directory `./pub/archive`; and `ftp.shsu.edu` [192.92.115.10], root directory `./tex-archive`. CTAN is also mirrored in `wuarchive.wustl.edu`. Other sites at which much (LA)TeX material can be obtained include

`labrea.standford.edu` [36.8.0.47]	`ymir.clairmont.edu` [134.173.4.23]
`sun.soe.clarkson.edu` [128.153.12.3]	`ftp.cs.ruu.nl` [131.211.80.17]

Once you begin to use the Internet to explore these and many other archives, you will initially be overwhelmed by the amount of material available for your use. However, after a bit or exploring, you will find that the Internet is an invaluable resource.

If you do not have access to the Internet, then you may still be able to obtain style files by joining TUG[1] or through your LATeX supplier.

8.2 Verbatim Text from an External File

It is better to include lengthy `verbatim` material into a document from an "external" file. If the material is placed in the `.TEX` file, TeX's internal memory is quickly consumed during compilation. If a `verbatim` extends more than two or three pages, you are likely to get an **out of memory** error. The `VERBFILE.STY` style, created by Tim Morgan, Adrian Clark, and Chris Bowley, offers a capability to read `verbatim` material from an external file and bring it into the document without exhausting TeX's memory. This LATeX style file defines two user-callable macros:

> `\verbatimfile{<filename>}`   for verbatim inclusion of a file
> `\verbatimlisting{<filename>}` for verbatim with line numbers

---

[1]The TeX User Group publishes an excellent newsletter which contains many useful hints, reviews, and news about (LA)TeX. To become a member, contact TeX Users Group, P.O. Box 869, Santa Barbara, CA 93102-0869, or e-mail them at `tug@tug.org`.

Here is an example of what is produced with `\verbatimfile{sub.lst}`:

```
DOUBLE PRECISION FUNCTION SVRT(ARG,ARG2,ERR)
IMPLICIT REAL*8(A-H,O-Z)
EXTERNAL FUN
COMMON ARG1
ARG1=ARG2
CALL GAUS8(FUN,0.DO,ARG,ERR,ANS,IERR)
SVRT=ANS
RETURN
END
```

Here is the same file imported with `\verbatimlisting{sub.lst}`:

```
1          DOUBLE PRECISION FUNCTION SVRT(ARG,ARG2,ERR)
2          IMPLICIT REAL*8(A-H,O-Z)
3          EXTERNAL FUN
4          COMMON ARG1
5          ARG1=ARG2
6          CALL GAUS8(FUN,0.DO,ARG,ERR,ANS,IERR)
7          SVRT=ANS
8          RETURN
9          END
```

8.3   Captions with Hanging Indents

In Section 5.3, it was seen that the default format that LaTeX uses for table or figure captions is far from ideal. First it extends across the full width of the page (column) in a nonindented paragraph form. Second, it leaves no space after the caption, so space must be manually inserted. A typical result is shown in Table 8.1.

Table 8.1: The discrete energies used for deriving the approximate line-beam response function. This is a long caption that extends over several lines.

i	E_i	i	E_i	i	E_i	i	E_i
1	0.02	3	0.04	5	0.08	7	0.2
2	0.03	4	0.06	6	0.10	8	0.4

The `HANGCAPTION.STY` style (of unknown parentage) defines a `\hangcaption` command that produces a hanging indent for the caption of a figure or table. Unlike LaTeX's `\caption` command, `\hangcaption` will honor a font size change, a very useful feature when placing small tables or figures side-by-side. It also automatically puts a small vertical space between the caption and table. Finally, a new \captionwidth command can be used to restrict the width of the label. With \hangcaption, Table 8.1 becomes

Table 8.2: The discrete energies used for deriving the approximate line-beam response function. This is a long caption that extends over several lines.

i	E_i	i	E_i	i	E_i	i	E_i
1	0.02	3	0.04	5	0.08	7	0.2
2	0.03	4	0.06	6	0.10	8	0.4

This was produced with

```
\begin{table}[htbp] \captionwidth 4.0in
  \centering
  \hangcaption{The discrete energies $E_i$ (MeV) used for
             deriving the approximate line-beam response
             function.  This is a long caption that extends
             over several lines. }   \label{t8b}
  \begin{tabular}{|rc|rc|rc|rc|}  \hline
     $i$ & $E_i$ & $i$ & $E_i$ & $i$ & $E_i$ & $i$ & $E_i$ \\
     \hline
        1 & 0.02 & 3 & 0.04 & 5 & 0.08 & 7 & 0.2 \\
        2 & 0.03 & 4 & 0.06 & 6 & 0.10 & 8 & 0.4 \\   \hline
  \end{tabular}
\end{table}
```

In Section 9.3, other more flexible methods are presented for customizing the caption for figures and tables.

8.4 More Flexible Numbering of Equations

The EQUATION style by Charles Karney extends the capabilities of LaTeX to allow greater flexibility in labeling and numbering equations. To use this style, include the equation style in the \documentstyle statement, for example,

\documentstyle[equation,12pt]{report}

In the following subsections, examples of the different equation environments provided by this style are given.

8.4.1   A Corrected eqnarray Environment

The `EQUATION.STY` modifies LaTeX's `eqnarray` and `eqnarray*` environments to correct the spacing around the $=$ sign. The command `\yesnumber` is used in `eqnarray*` to generate an equation number, while `\nonumber` prevents an automatic equation number in the `eqnarray` environment. Here is an example.

$$
\begin{aligned}
a &= b \\
&+ c \\
&+ d \\
&+ e \quad (8.1)
\end{aligned}
$$

```
\begin{eqnarray*}
   a &=& b \\
     & & + c \\
     & & + d \\
     & & + e \yesnumber
\end{eqnarray*}
```

8.4.2   The eqalign Environment

The new `eqalign` environment is like plain TeX's `\eqalign` command. Note that this environment must be embedded in `\begin{equation}` ... `\end{equation}` (or its equivalent).

$$
\begin{aligned}
a &= b, \\
c &= d.
\end{aligned} \quad (8.2)
$$

```
\begin{equation}
   \begin{eqalign}
      a &= b, \\
      c &= d.
   \end{eqalign}
\end{equation}
```

8.4.3   The eqalignno Environment

`EQUATION.STY`'s `eqalignno` environment is just like TeX's `\eqalignno` command. However, no `\begin{equation}` ... `\end{equation}` is needed. The command `\nonumber` is used to suppress the equation number. The environment `eqalignno*` is the same as `eqalignno` except that automatic equation numbers are suppressed (unless a `\yesnumber` appears).

$$
\begin{aligned}
a &= b, \quad (8.3) \\
c &= d. \quad (8.4)
\end{aligned}
$$

```
\begin{eqalignno}
   a &= b, \label{eqalign1}\\
   c &= d. \label{eqalign2}
\end{eqalignno}
```

8.4.4 The `eqaligntwo` Environment

The `eqaligntwo` environment is a two-equation per line equivalent of the `eqalignno` environment. The `eqaligntwo*` environment is similar except that automatic equation numbering is suppressed.

$$a = b, \qquad x = y, \qquad (8.5)$$
$$c = d, \qquad z = w. \qquad (8.6)$$

```
\begin{eqaligntwo}
  a &= b, & x &= y, \label{e1} \\
  c &= d, & z &= w. \label{e2}
\end{eqaligntwo}
```

8.4.5 The `cases` Environment

The `cases` environment is just like plain TeX's `\cases` command. Note that this environment must be embedded in `\begin{equation}` ... `\end{equation}` (or its equivalent). The first column is treated as math and the second column as text.

$$u(x) = \begin{cases} 0, & \text{for } x < 0, \\ 1, & \text{for } x \geq 0. \end{cases} \qquad (8.7)$$

```
\begin{equation}
  u(x) =
    \begin{cases}
      0, & for $x < 0$,
      1, & for $x \ge 0$.
    \end{cases}
\end{equation}
```

8.4.6 The `subequations` Environment

The EQUATION style also incorporates Stephen Gildea's `subequations` environment. With this environment you can refer both to the overall set of equations and to individual subequations in it.

$$a = b, \qquad (8.8a)$$
$$c = d, \qquad (8.8b)$$

and some lines of text placed between the subequations ...

$$e = f. \qquad (8.8c)$$

```
\begin{subequations} \label{foo}
  \begin{eqalignno}
    a &= b, \label{foo-a} \\
    c &= d, \label{foo-b}
  \end{eqalignno}
  and some lines of text placed
  between the subequations ...
  \begin{equation}
    e = f. \label{foo-c}
  \end{equation}
\end{subequations}
```

With this environment `Eqs.~(\ref{foo})` produces Eqs. (8.8) while the subequation reference `Eq.~(\ref{foo-a})` produces Eq. (8.8a), `Eq.~(\ref{foo-b})` produces Eq. (8.8b), and `Eq.~(\ref{foo-c})` produces Eq. (8.8c).

8.5   Wrapping Text around a Figure: I

Wrapping text around figures in LaTeX is difficult. However, the `WRAPFIG.STY` style, written by Donald Arseneau, allows you to place a figure of a specified width on the left or right of the page and have the text flow around it. `WRAPFIG` will try to wrap text around the figure, leaving a gap of `\columsep` by producing a number of short lines of text. `WRAPFIG` calculates the number of short lines

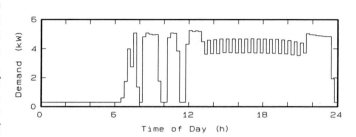

Figure 8.1: Example load profile

needed based on the height of the figure plus the length `\intextsep`. You can override this guess by giving the optional argument specifying the number of shortened lines (counting each displayed equation as 3 lines). `WRAPFIG` will not move a wrapped figure to the best place, so it is up to you to position it well. Any changes to the document can ruin your careful positioning, so wrapped figures should be positioned just before printing a final copy.

Here are some hints for good placement. (1) The `wrapfigure` environment should be placed so as to not run over a page boundary. (2) Only ordinary text should have to flow past the figure (no section titles) although equations are acceptable if they fit. (3) Although it is convenient to give `\begin{wrapfigure}` just after a paragraph has ended, if you want to start in the middle of a paragraph, you must put the environment between two words where there is a natural line break (such as "...on the" and "left or right..." in the above example).

At the point in the text where you wish to place a wrapped figure, issue the following:

```
\begin{wrapfigure}[no. narrow lines] {r or l} {fig. width}
     <figure specification>
     [\caption{...}  \label{...}]
\end{wrapfigure}
```

Figure 8.1 was inserted in its paragraph with the following commands:

```
... to place a figure of a specified width on the
\begin{wrapfigure}{r}{3.7in}
     \vspace{1.5in}
```

```
        \special{pcl:facload.pcl}
        \caption{An example load profile} \label{f8a}
\end{wrapfigure}
        left or right of the page and have the text ...
```

There are a few restrictions on the use of WRAPFIG.STY. First, the wrapfigure environment should not be used inside another environment (for example, a list). There should be a only one wrapped figure per paragraph. Finally, wrapped figures do not float and hence they may get out of sequence with other floating figures.

8.6   Wrapping Text around a Figure: II

Here is another way to wrap text around a figure, table, or any other object. The style WRAPFIG.STY discussed in the previous section allows you to place a figure of a specified width on the left or right of a paragraph if the user selects the proper line break at which the "short lines" are to begin.   A more sophisticated way to wrap text around figures or tables is to use the style

Figure 8.2: Sample figure

file PICINPAR.STY created by Friedhelm Sowa. Here is a simple figure (created in the picture environment) that is placed to the right of the paragraph after the first two full lines. Notice that PICINPAR calculates the number of short lines needed and wraps the text accordingly. Moreover, the user does not have to determine after what word the short lines begin!

The style PICINPAR provides three environments: (1) figwindow for embedding figures with a caption into a paragraph, (2) tabwindow for placing tables with a caption into a paragraph, and (3) window for putting anything into a display box without placing a table or figure caption beneath. Into these environments goes the text of the paragraph as well. The general syntax for \figwindow is (the others are similar)

\figwindow[*no. top long lines*,|l,r,c|,{*picture*},{*caption*}]

In this command l,r, or c refers to left, right, or center justification. For example, the first paragraph in this section was created with

```
\begin{figwindow}[2,r,{ \unitlength 1in
   \begin{picture}(3,1.2)
      \put(0.7,0.7){\circle*{0.2}}     \put(0.7,0.7){\circle{1.2}}
      \put(0.7,0.7){\vector(0,1){0.4}} \put(2.5,0.7){\circle*{0.5}}
   \end{picture}
   \vspace{-.2in}},{Sample figure}]  %--move caption up a bit
   Here is another way to wrap ... the short lines begin!
\end{figwindow}
```

The command \begin{tabwindow}...\end{tabwindow} can be used to place a table either to the left or right or centered in a paragraph. In fact, several

1	ABC	12:0
2	DEF	11:1
3	HIJ	10:2
4	KLM	9:3
5	1. XYZ	8:4

Table 8.3: Example

paragraphs can be placed between the \begin{tabwindow} ...\end{tabwindow} so that the table window spans multiple paragraphs as in this example.

The only problem that seems to be unusual with PICINPAR is that the table caption is placed *under* the table in the European fashion. (Actually, this is not too surprising since Sowa is from Germany.) You might be tempted to leave the caption argument of the tabwindow environment empty to avoid any caption at all. However, this does not work since the "Table xx:" is still added below the table. To avoid any caption at all, simply use the plain window environment.

This table example was created by the following input:

```
\begin{tabwindow}[2,1,{\begin{tabular}[t]{|r|l|r@{:}l|}
                    ...
              \end{tabular}},{Example}]
      The command ... use the {\tt window} environment.
\end{tabwindow}
```

A .PCL file created externally by some graphics programs can also be embedded into a paragraph with PICINPAR. This is an example done with LATEX's \special command. Here we are trying to place the figure in the center of the paragraph. However, with ment, there is no way the figure. We must cre- PCL file that is just the takes considerable trial most never would we try in the center of a para- cult for the eye to bridge ble. All in all, this capa- not seem to be very use- is when the graph or ta- width of the paragraph.

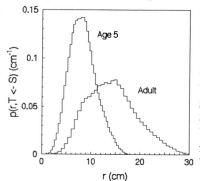

the figwindow environ- to specify the width of ate a the "space" for the right size. This often and error. However, al- to place a figure or table graph since it is diffi- across the graphic or ta- bility of PICINPAR does ful. The one exception ble occupies the whole A full-width graphic can

be more easily inserted into a paragraph using the methods discussed in Chapter 6. This paragraph which contains an imbedded central figure was created with

```
\begin{window}[3,c,{
  \vadjust{\vskip 1.95in {\hbox to 1.95in
  {\special{pcl:ptpair.pcl}\hfill}}}},{}]
    A {\tt .PCL} file created externally by some ...
\end{window}
```

8.7   Customizing Headers and Footers

This `FANCYHDS.STY` style, created by Piet van Oostrum, allows you to customize page headers and footers in an easy way. The following description is taken almost verbatim from the documentation that comes with `FANCYHDS`. This style combines features that were separately available in other page styles and allows you to create quite complex headers and footers for your document.

With `FANCYHDS` you can define (1) three-part headers and footers, (2) rules in headers and footers, (3) headers and footers wider than `\textwidth`, (4) multiline headers and footers, (5) separate headers and footers for even and odd pages, and (6) separate headers and footers for chapter pages.

To use this page style, you must include `fancyhds` as a style option in the `\documentstyle` declaration at the beginning of your LaTeX file. You must also issue the `\pagestyle{fancy}` command in the preamble after you have made any changes you want to `\textwidth`. The page layout assumed by `FANCYHDS` is as follows:

The L-fields will be left adjusted, the C-fields centered, and the R-fields right justified. Each of the six fields and the two rules can be defined separately.

8.7.1   Simple Use

The header and footer fields can be defined by commands `\lhead{LHEAD}` and so on for the other fields. If the field depends on something in the document (for example, section titles), you must in general use the `\markboth` and `\markright` commands; otherwise, a title may end on the wrong page. You can do this by redefining the commands `\chaptermark`, `\sectionmark`, and so on (see the examples in Section 8.7.8). The defaults for these marks are as in the standard page styles. The marks can be put into a header or footer field by referencing `\leftmark` and `\rightmark`.

8.7.2 Rules in Header and Footer

The thickness of the rules below the header and above the footer can be changed by redefining the length parameter `\headrulewidth` (default 0.4 point) and the length parameter `\footrulewidth` (default 0). These may be redefined by the `\setlength` command. A thickness of 0 point makes the rule invisible. If you want to make more complicated changes, you have to redefine the commands `\headrule` and/or `\footrule`.

For example, if you want a dotted line rather than a ruler, place the following command in the preamble:

```
\renewcommand{\headrule}{\vbox to 0pt{\hbox to\headwidth
                                     {\dotfill}\vss}}
```

8.7.3 Headers and Footers Wider Than the Text

The headers and footers are set in a box of width `\headwidth`. The default for this is the value of `\textwidth`. You can make it wider (or smaller) by redefining `\headwidth` with the `\setlength` or `\addtolength` command. The headers and footers will extend out of the page on the same side as the marginal notes. For example, to include the marginal notes, add both `\marginparsep` and `\marginparwidth` to `\headwidth`.

8.7.4 Multiline Headers and Footers

Each of the six fields is set in an appropriate `\parbox`, so you can put a multiline part in it with the `\\` command. It is also possible to put extra space in it with the `\vspace` command. Note that if you do this you will probably have to increase the `\headheight` or `\footskip` lengths.

8.7.5 Headers and Footers for Even and Odd Pages

If you want the headers and footers to be different on even- and odd-numbered pages in the *twoside* style, the field-defining macros can be given an optional argument, to be used on even-numbered pages, like `\lhead[EVEN-LHEAD]{ODD-LHEAD}`.

8.7.6 Separate Headers and Footers for Chapter Pages

LaTeX gives a \thispagestyle{plain} command for the first page of the document, the first page of each chapter and a couple of other pages. It might be incompatible with your page style. In this case you can use a slightly different version of the page style, called \pagestyle{fancyplain}. This page style redefines the page style "plain" to also use page style "fancy" with the following modifications:

- The thicknesses of the rules is defined by \plainheadrulewidth and \plainfootrulewidth (both default 0).

- The six fields may be defined separately for the plain pages by giving them the value \fancyplain{PLAIN-VALUE}{NORMAL-VALUE}. This construct may be used in both the optional argument and the normal argument.

  Thus \lhead[\fancyplain{F1}{F2}]{\fancyplain{F3}{F4}} specifies the LHEAD value in a two-sided document:

  ▷ F1 on an even-numbered "plain" page
  ▷ F2 on an even-numbered normal page
  ▷ F3 on an odd-numbered "plain" page
  ▷ F4 on an odd-numbered normal page

8.7.7 Defaults

```
\headrulewidth          0.4pt
\footrulewidth          0pt
\plainheadrulewidth     0pt
\plainfootrulewidth     0pt
%empty on ``plain'', \rightmark on even, \leftmark on odd pages
\lhead[\fancyplain{}{\sl\rightmark}]{\fancyplain{}{\sl\leftmark}}
\chead{}
%empty on ``plain'', \leftmark on even, \rightmark on odd pages
\rhead[\fancyplain{}{\sl\leftmark}]{\fancyplain{}{\sl\rightmark}}
\lfoot{}
\cfoot{\rm\thepage} % page number
\rfoot{}
```

8.7.8 Section Titles in the Headers and Footers

You can't just change the header and/or footer fields in the middle of some text (for example, after a section header), because TeX may have processed a bit more text before deciding to make up the page. It may have passed a section beginning, causing the wrong title on the page. TeX has a mechanism called 'marks' to solve this

problem. There is in LaTeX a \leftmark and a \rightmark. Usually, \leftmark
is a chapter title and \rightmark is a section title. To set the marks there are two
commands: \markboth{L}{R} sets the \leftmark to L and the rightmark to R, and
\rightmark{R} sets only the rightmark to R. The default definitions of \section,
and so on, do this already for you. Consider this example.

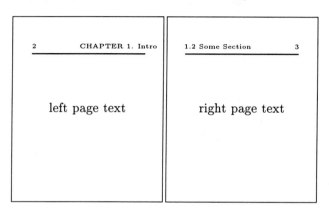

This header format can be easily achieved with FANCYHDS by putting the following
in the document preamble.

```
\pagestyle{fancy}
\setlength{\headrulewidth}{1pt}
\lhead[\rm\thepage]{\rm\rightmark}
\rhead[\sl\leftmark]{\rm\thepage}
```

The last two lines specify that, on even pages (the [ ] parts), the left header is
the page number and right header is \leftmark, which is the chapter title because
LaTeX makes that the left argument of \markboth (see page 162 of Lamport's LaTeX
book). On odd pages (the { } parts), the left header is \rightmark, which is the
last section title because LaTeX makes that the argument to \markright, and the
right header is the page number.

Now suppose you don't want the section number and you want the section title
in uppercase: You add the following to your preamble:

```
\renewcommand{\sectionmark}[1]{\markright{\uppercase{#1}}}
```

Or if you don't want the chapter number, but only the chapter title (not in uppercase):

```
\renewcommand{\chaptermark}[1]{\markboth{#1}{ }}
```

Note that the parameter in both cases is the section or chapter title.

8.8 Frames and Boxes

The style file `FANCYBOX.STY`, created by Timothy Van Zandt, allows you to use all kinds of boxes in a document. Besides creating special commands for boxes, many special macros are defined for handling verbatim text, using special list environments, placing frames around pages, and positioning text inside various boxes (including rotating text). The document that comes with `FANCYBOX` is an excellent tutorial on how to write macros and special environments. In the following, only a few of the special features are demonstrated.

8.8.1 Fancy Boxes

`FANCYBOX` defines the following variants of the LaTeX `\fbox` command: `\shadowbox`, `\doublebox`, `\ovalbox` (using `\thinlines`), and `\Ovalbox` (using `\thicklines`). Here are examples:

LaTeX (shadowbox)	`\shadowbox{\large\bf \LaTeX}`
LaTeX (doublebox)	`\doublebox{\large\bf \LaTeX}`
LaTeX (ovalbox)	`\ovalbox{\large\bf \LaTeX}`
LaTeX (Ovalbox)	`\Ovalbox{\large\bf \LaTeX}`

The distance between the box and the frame is `\fboxsep`, as with LaTeX's `\fbox` command. The commands use other parameters as well:

`\shadowbox`: The width of the frame is `\fboxrule` (the same as with `\fbox`). The width of the shadow is `\shadowsize` (default: 4pt).

`\doublebox`: The width of the inner frame is .75`\fboxrule`, and the width of the outer frame is 1.5`\fboxrule`. The distance between the two frames is 1.5`\fboxrule` plus .5pt.

`\ovalbox`: The width of the frame is set by the `\thinlines` declaration. The diameter of the corner arcs is set with the `\cornersize{<num}`

to <num> times the lesser of the width and height of the box. An alternative command [\cornersize*{<dim>}] sets the diameter of the corner arcs approximately to <dim>. This is all approximate, because LaTeX has a limited range of arc sizes to choose from. The default is \cornersize{.5}.

\Ovalbox: This is like \ovalbox, except that the width of the lines is set by the \thicklines declaration.

There are no analogs to LaTeX's \framebox command, which has various optional arguments not supported by \fbox. You can get the exact same functionality by putting the argument of the preceding framing commands in a \makebox.

There is also a variant \fancyoval of LaTeX's \oval picture object. The difference is that \oval always makes the diameter of the corner arcs as large as possible, and \fancyoval uses the \cornersize command to set the diameter.

8.8.2   Large Frames

One of the more spectacular features (but of limited utility) is FANCYBOX's ability to put frames around an entire page or portion of a page. The following commands

$$\text{\textbackslash fancyput*}(x,y)\{LR\ stuff\} \quad \text{and} \quad \text{\textbackslash thisfancyput*}(x,y)\{LR\ stuff\}$$

are much like the \put commands in a LaTeX picture environment whose origin is 1 inch down and to the right of the top-left corner of the page. The only differences are that (1) that any LR-mode material is permitted (including LaTeX picture environment, of course), (2) the coordinate is optional and (0pt,0pt) is substituted by default, and (3) if the coordinate is included, you *must* specify the units. The command \thisfancyput affects only the current page, and is a global declaration (analogous to \thispagestyle). If you include the optional *, then the command adds to, rather than replaces, other things that have been inserted with \fancyput or \thisfancyput.

These commands are particularly useful for framing all of a page, because the frame is positioned with respect to the physical page and not with respect to the text on the page. The oval around this section was created with

```
\thisfancyput(3.25in,-4.5in){\setlength{\unitlength}{1in}
\fancyoval(6.5,10.25)}
```

Warning: The commands described in this section change LaTeX's output routine and may not work with document styles that do the same. Also, bad arguments can cause serious errors with uninformative error messages.

8.9 Multicolumns of Text

The style MULTICOLS.STY, written by Frank Mittelbach, allows switching between a one-column and multicolumn format on the same page. Footnotes are handled correctly (for the most part), but will be placed at the bottom of the page and not under each column. LaTeX's float mechanism, however, is partly disabled in the current implementation. In the present version (1.4m), only page-wide floats (that is, *-forms) can be used within the scope of the environment.

An extensive document describing the many features of this style accompanies MULTICOLS.STY. With Mittelbach's kind permission, a small portion of his documentation is printed below. This extract, reproduced almost verbatim, gives most of the instructions for the use of the multicols environment. Only the formatting has been changed to demonstrate the flexibility of multicols

8.9.1 The User Interface

To use the environment one simply says

```
\begin{multicols}{⟨number⟩}
        ⟨multicolumn text⟩
\end{multicols}
```

where ⟨*number*⟩ is the required number of columns and ⟨*multicolumn text*⟩ may contain arbitrary LaTeX commands, except that floats and marginpars are not allowed in the current implementation.[2]

As its first action, the multicols environment measures the current page to determine whether there is enough room for some portion of multicolumn output. This is controlled by the ⟨*dimen*⟩ variable \premulticols which can be changed by the user with ordinary LaTeX commands. If the space is less than \premulticols, a new page is started. Otherwise, a \vskip of \multicolsep is added.[3]

When the end of the multicols environment is encountered, an analogous mechanism is employed, but now we test whether there is a space larger than \postmulticols available. Again we add \multicolsep or start a new page.

It is often convenient to spread some text over all columns, just before the multicolumn output, without any page break in between. To achieve this the multicols environment has an optional second argument which can be used for this purpose. For example, the text you are now reading was started with

```
\begin{multicols}{3}
    [\section{The User Interface}] ...
```

If such text is unusually long (or short) the value of \premulticols might need adjusting to prevent a bad page break. We therefore provide a third argument which can be used to overwrite the default value of \premulticols just for this occasion. So if you want to combine some longer single column text with a multicols environment you could write

```
\begin{multicols}{3}
    [\section{Index}
        This index contains ...] [6cm]
        ...
```

Separation of the columns with vertical rules is achieved by setting the parameter \columnseprule to some positive value. In this article a value of .4pt is used.

Since narrow columns tend to need adjustments in interline spacing we also provide a ⟨*skip*⟩ parameter called \multicolbaselineskip which is added to the \baselineskip parameter inside the multicols environment. Please use

---

[2] To implement floats one has to reimplement the whole LaTeX output routine.

[3] Actually the added space may be less because we use \addvspace (see the LaTeX manual for further information about this command).

this parameter with care or leave it alone; it is intended only for style file designers since even small changes might produce totally unexpected changes to your document.

8.9.2 Balancing Columns

Besides the previously mentioned parameters, some others are provided to influence the layout of the columns generated.

Paragraphing in TEX is controlled by several parameters. One of the most important is called \tolerance: this controls the allowed 'looseness' (i.e. the amount of blank space between words). Its default value is 200 (the LATEX \fussy) which is too small for narrow columns. On the other hand the \sloppy declaration (which sets \tolerance to 10000 = ∞) is too large, allowing really bad spacing.[4]

We therefore use a \multicoltolerance parameter for the \tolerance value inside the multicols environment. Its default value is 9999 which is less than infinity but 'bad' enough for most paragraphs in a multicolumn environment. Changing its value should be done outside the multicols environment. Since \tolerance is set to \multicoltolerance at the beginning of every multicols environment one can locally overwrite this default by assigning \tolerance␣=␣⟨desired value⟩. There also exists a \multicolpretolerance parameter holding the value for \pretolerance within a multicols environment. Both parameters are usually used only by style designers.

Generation of multicolumn output can be divided into two parts. In the first part we are collecting material for a page, shipping it out, collecting material for the next page, and so on. As a second step, balancing will be done when the end of the multicols environment is reached. In the first step TEX might consider more material while finding the final columns than it actually uses when shipping out the page. This might cause a problem if a footnote is encountered in the part of the input considered, but not used, on the current page. In this case the footnote might show up on the current page, while the footnotemark corresponding to this footnote might be set on the next one.[5] Therefore the multicols environment gives a warning message[6] whenever it is unable to use all the material considered so far.

If you don't use footnotes too often the chances of something actually going wrong are very slim, but if this happens you can help TEX by using a \pagebreak command in the final document. Another way to influence the behavior of TEX in this respect is given by the counter variable 'collectmore'. If you use the \setcounter declaration to set this counter to ⟨number⟩, TEX will consider ⟨number⟩ more (or less) lines before making its final decision. So a value of −1 may solve all your problems at the cost of slightly less optimal columns.

In the second step (balancing columns) we have other bells and whistles. First of all you can say \raggedcolumns if you don't want the bottom lines to be aligned. The default is \flushcolumns, so TEX will normally try to align both the top and bottom baselines of all columns.

Additionally you can set another counter, the 'unbalance' counter, to some positive ⟨number⟩. This will make all but the rightmost column ⟨number⟩ of lines longer than they would normally have been. 'Lines' in this context refer to normal text lines (i.e. one \baselineskip apart); thus, if your columns contain displays, for example, you may need a higher ⟨number⟩ to shift something from one column into another.

Unlike 'collectmore,' the 'unbalance' counter is reset to zero at the end of the environment so it only applies to one multicols environment.

The two methods may be combined but I suggest using these features only when fine tuning important publications.

---

[4]Look at the next paragraph, it was set with the \sloppy declaration.

[5]The reason behind this behavior is the asynchronous character of the TEX *page_builder*. However, this could be avoided by defining very complicated output routines which don't use TEX primitives like \insert but do everything by hand.

[6]This message will be generated even if there are no footnotes in this part of the text.

8.9.3 Floats

Within the multicols environment the usual star float commands are available but their function is somewhat different as in the two-column mode of standard LaTeX. Starred floats, e.g., `figure*`, denote page wide floats that are handled in a similar fashion as normal floats outside the multicols environment. However, they will never show up on the page where they are encountered. In other words, one can influence their placement by specifying a combination of t, b, and/or p in their optional argument, but h doesn't work because the first possible place is the top of the next page. One should also note, that this means that their placement behavior is determined by the values of `\topfraction`, etc. rather than by `\dbl....`

8.9.4 Warnings

Under certain circumstances the use of the multicols environment may result in some warnings from TeX or LaTeX. Here is a list of the important ones and the possible cause:

`Underfull \hbox (badness ...)`

As the columns are often very narrow TeX wasn't able to find a good way to break the paragraph. Underfull denotes a loose line but as long the badness value is below 10000 the result is probably acceptable.

`Underfull \vbox ... while \outputis active`

If a column contains a character with an unusual depth (for example, a '(' in the bottom line), then this message may show up. It usually is insignificant if not more than a few points.

`LaTeX Warning: I moved some lines to the next page`

As mentioned above, multicols sometimes screws up the footnote numbering. As a precaution, whenever there is a footnote on a page and where multicols had to leave a remainder for the following page this warning appears. Check the footnote numbering on this page. If it turns out that it is wrong you have to break the page manually using `\newpage` or `\pagebreak[..]`.

`Floats and marginpars not allowed inside 'multicols' environment!`

This message appears if you try to use the `\marginpar` command or an unstarred version of the figure or table environment. Such floats will disappear!

Chapter 9

Macros and Miscellaneous Tricks

In the previous chapters, many macros for performing special tricks in LaTeX were presented with little explanation of how and why they work. Development of the skills necessary to create elaborate macros often requires an understanding of (LA)TeX's inner workings that few of us have the time (or desire) to obtain. However, as demonstrated by the many macro examples used in this book, LaTeX allows us to use macros created by others without the need to understand them fully. Often only a superficial knowledge of (LA)TeX commands is sufficient to make minor modifications in a particular macro to alter what it does.

In this chapter, brief explanations are given of some of the commands used in the earlier macro examples. This introduction to the basics of macro programming for (LA)TeX is intended mainly to provide the reader with a very rudimentary understanding of how macro and style files are written. To gain a detailed knowledge about how to write macros and style files from scratch, there is no substitute for many careful readings of D. L. Knuth's *The TeXbook* (Addison-Wesley, New York, NY, 1990).

Later in this chapter, a series of recipes or tricks for doing several nonstandard things with LaTeX is presented. For the most part, these tricks have been gleaned from various network sources, notably UKHAX, TUG Newsletters, TEXHAX, and NetNews. This later resource, the Internet News Service, has a discussion group `comp.text.tex` which is an excellent place to pick up various tricks and to ask for help from a worldwide community of (LA)TeX experts.

9.1 Basics of Macro Programming

LATEX is a large collection of macros (about 11,000 lines) built using the rich command set of TEX. These macros are defined in four files: (1) `lplain.tex` (a minor modification of TEX's `plain.tex`, which is used for normal TEX documents), (2) `latex.tex` (the file containing the bulk of LATEX's macros), (3) `lfonts.tex` (which defines LATEX's fonts and their commands), and (4) `hyphen.tex` (which defines American hyphenation patterns). These four files are compiled to produce a binary file `lplain.fmt` that TEX can load quickly whenever you want to LATEX your document. If you want to see how LATEX does a particular task, the macro for the task is probably to be found in `latex.tex`. This is an excellent file to browse through to become more familiar with creating macros and style files.

LATEX also has four *primary* style files: `letter`, `report`, `article`, and `book` that define macros for special commands used by these four styles (for example, the section heading commands). If you want to change how LATEX formats, for example, the section heading command, you extract the macro for the section heading from the appropriate `.STY` file and modify it (see Section 9.2.3).

9.1.1 Defining New Commands

The key to creating new macros and styles for LATEX is to define new commands. A command name begins with a backslash \ and an alphabetic label (no numbers!). The command names used by (LA)TEX use only the lowercase alphabetic characters, and to avoid conflicts by inadvertently choosing a command name that is the same as an existing (LA)TEX command name, it is a good idea to use some uppercase alphabetic letters in your command names, for example, `\Mycmd`.

Creating New Commands with LATEX

LATEX's `\newcommand` may be used to define a new command. Its syntax is

$$\texttt{\textbackslash newcommand\{\textbackslash}\textit{cmdname}\texttt{\}[}\textit{numargs}\texttt{]\{}\textit{cmddefn}\texttt{\}}$$

where *cmdname* is the command name, [*noargs*] is optional and gives the number of arguments for the command (a maximum of nine), and *cmddefn* is the text string that defines the command. If *cmdname* is the name of an existing command, LATEX will produce an error message. Here are a couple of examples.

```
\newcommand{\keff}{$k_{\!\mbox{\scriptsize \em eff}}$}
\newcommand{\Nuclide}[2]{${}^{#2}$#1}
```

With these macros (placed either in the preamble or in the document itself before they are first used), `\keff` will produce k_{eff} and `\Nuclide{U}{235}` gives ^{235}U.

To change an existing command, LaTeX provides \renewcommand. Its syntax and use are the same as that of \newcommand. For example, the vertical space normally made by \bigskip can be increased by redefining this command as

$$\renewcommand\{\bigskip\}\{\vspace\{3cm\}\}$$

Creating New Commands with TeX

TeX provides the \def command to define new commands. It is used as

$$\def\cmdname\#1\#2\#3...\{cmddefn\}$$

where the argument specifiers #1#2#3... are used only if *cmddefn* needs arguments. This command may be used in LaTeX but, unlike LaTeX's \newcommand, it does not check to see if \cmdname is already used. Here's how the \keff and \Nuclide macro (previously defined with \newcommand) could be defined using the \def command.

```
\def\keff{$k_{\!\mbox{\scriptsize \em eff}}$\ }
\def\Nuclide#1#2{${}^{#2}$#1}
```

The argument list #1#2#3... can specify up to nine arguments and must be in increasing order, although they can be used in any order in *cmddefn*.

The *cmddefn* string, which defines the new command, can be spread over several lines, but no blank lines (or \par commands) may appear in the definition. If blank lines or \par are needed in *cmddefn*, use the compound \long\def command. Other modifiers to the \def command include \outer, to restrict the use of the command to the outermost level of TeX processing, and \global, to enable the continued operation of the command even outside the group in which it was invoked.

Internal @ Commands

In the definition of a large macro or style, often commands are used only as local or *internal* commands. By convention, these command names contain the @ character to avoid inadvertent conflicts with a command name you might choose. By contrast, commands to be used in a document are *external* commands and are named only with letters.

To enforce this convention, LaTeX will accept commands containing the @ symbol only in style files loaded as style options in the \documentstyle command. LaTeX normally refuses to accept such commands in the document itself. However, you can force LaTeX to accept these internal commands inside your document by preceding their appearance with the command \makeatletter, which causes @ to be treated as an ordinary character. The \makeatother command reestablishes the normal convention. Many macros suggested in earlier chapters contain commands with the

@ symbol, and to include them in a document's preamble, it is necessary to begin them with \makeatletter and to end them with \makeatother.

9.1.2 Some Commands Used in Macros

In the definition of new commands and macros, several TEX commands are frequently used. In this section a brief overview of some of the more important commands is presented.

Assignment Statement

The TEX assignment statement \let*newcommand*=*oldcommand* creates a new command *newcommand* that has exactly the same definition as the command *oldcommand*.

Conditional Statements

To allow a macro to change the control flow, TEX uses the following conditional statements:

> \if*condition   true-commands* \fi
> \if*condition   true-commands* \else *false-commands* \fi

where the *true-commands* (*false-commands*) are executed if *condition* is true (false). Many *conditions* are predefined, such as \ifodd*number*, \ifdim, \ifcase*number*, and \ifnum.

There are also logical switches that may be defined by the user. The command \newif\if*myswitch* defines three control sequences: (1) *myswitch*true to set *myswitch* to true, (2) *myswitch*false to set *myswitch* to false, and (3) \if*myswitch true-commands* \else *false-commands* \fi.

LATEX has defined a very useful conditional \ifthenelse command. To use this command the document style option ifthen must be specified. The syntax of this command is

> \ifthenelse{*test*}{*true-commands*}{*false-commands*}

The *test* argument allows easy construction of logical conditions using two basic constructions. The first has the form *number1 rel number2*, where *rel* is one of < = >. Such simple tests may be combined into complex Boolean expressions using \and, \not, \or, and parentheses \(and \). The second construction has the form \equal{*cmds1*}{*cmds2*}. Here *cmds1* and *cmds2* are sets of macro calls that produce a true condition only if they produce identical results after expansion.

Looping

TEX commands can be recursive, that is, they can call themselves thereby allowing them to be repeated many times until some terminating condition is satisfied. TEX also has a `\loop` command that allows iterative execution of macros. This command has the syntax

$$\texttt{\textbackslash loop} \quad \textit{pre-test-cmds} \quad \texttt{\textbackslash if} \quad \textit{condition} \quad \textit{post-test-cmds} \quad \texttt{\textbackslash repeat}$$

The *pre-test-cmds* are executed first. Then the *condition* is evaluated, and, if *condition* is true, the *post-test-cmds* are executed and the loop is begun again. If *condition* is false, execution continues with the commands after `\repeat`.

LATEX has also defined the following easy-to-use looping command:

$$\texttt{\textbackslash whiledo}\{\textit{test}\}\{\textit{while-commands}\}$$

where the logical *test* is constructed in the same manner as used for the *test* condition in the `\ifthenelse` LATEX command described previously. To use this command the document style option `ifthen` must first be specified.

Groupings

The macro commands used in the arguments of looping and conditional statements can be confined to groups with the usual braces { and } or with the pair of commands `\begingroup` and `\endgroup`. These group delimiters *must* appear in matched pairs.

Sometimes a macro definition requires an unmatched group delimiter. For this purpose, TEX has the special commands `\bgroup` (for a "begin group") and `\egroup` (for an "end group"), which need not appear in matched pairs.

9.2   Page Layout Tricks

9.2.1   Macro for Side-by-Side Displays

Sometimes you will want to produce side-by-side displays of material such as

$$
\begin{array}{cc}
a+b+c & x-y \\
a+b & z \\
a & xyz
\end{array}
$$

```
$\begin{array}{cc}
a+b+c  &  x-y  \\
a+b    &  z    \\
a      &  xyz
\end{array}$
```

This was produced by

```
\egstart
    ..... (material for left minipage)
\egmid
    ..... (material for right minipage)
\egend
```

The \egstart, \egmid, \egend commands are defined by the following macros placed in the preamble of your document:

```
%=========== Macro for LaTeX Side-by-Side Minipages ===========
\newlength{\egwidth}\setlength{\egwidth}{0.45\textwidth}
\newenvironment{eg}%
  {\begin{list}{}{\setlength{\leftmargin}{0.05\textwidth}%
  \setlength{\rightmargin}{\leftmargin}}\item[]\footnotesize}%
  {\end{list}}
\newenvironment{egbox}%
  {\begin{minipage}[t]{\egwidth}}%
  {\end{minipage}}
\newcommand{\egstart}{\begin{eg}\begin{egbox}}
\newcommand{\egmid}{\end{egbox}\hfill\begin{egbox}}
\newcommand{\egend}{\end{egbox}\end{eg}}
%==============================================================
```

9.2.2 Underlining and Striking out Text

The LaTeX command \underline only works for a small portion of text since it puts the text into an \hbox that cannot be broken at the end of a line. A very cumbersome way to get around this limitation is to underline each word and interword space separately as in

```
\underbar{this}\underbar{\ }\underbar{will}\underbar{\ }%
\underbar{do}\underbar{\ }\underbar{the}\underbar{\ }\underbar{job}.
```

Knuth wrote in the TeXbook "If you really want underlined text, it's best to have a special font in which all the letters are underlined." Until such fonts become available, here are two useful macros, one for underlining and the other for striking out text. Although not perfect, they are adequate for drafts. To underline text, use \underlinewords{*text*}, and to strike out text, use \stikeoutwords{*text*}. Note: The *text* cannot have a paragraph break in it. To underline multiple paragraphs, place each paragraph in its own \underlinewords command.

```
%=========== Macros for Underlining and Striking Out ===========
%-- by Michael Barr
\def\underlinewords#1{%
  \def\stuff{#1 }\leavevmode\expandafter\ulword\stuff * }
  \def\ulword#1 {\def\one{#1} \ifx\one\aster\let\next\relax
  \else\vtop{\hbox{\strut#1}\hrule\relax}
```

```
      \let\next\ulword\fi\next}
\def\strikeoutwords#1{%
      \def\stuff{#1 }\leavevmode\expandafter\soword\stuff * }
      \def\soword#1 {\def\one{#1} \ifx\one\aster\let\next\relax
      \else\vtop{\hbox{\strut#1}\kern-.5\baselineskip\hrule\relax}
      \let\next\soword\fi\next}
\def\aster{*}
%=============================================================
```

9.2.3   San Serif Section Headings

The normal LaTeX chapter and section headings are viewed by many as being too large and too assertive. The format for a 10pt book document's headings, for example, is defined in LaTeX's BOOK.STY and BK10.STY style files. The style file SSHDBK10.STY below is extracted from these style files and modified to produce sans serif headings at a slightly reduced size (for example, huge in place of Huge). The changes to the original definitions are indicated by ˆˆˆˆ in the comment lines. This style file can be used with other document styles and should be specified as a style option in the \documentstyle command. Alternatively, you could put \makeatletter at the beginning and \makeatother at the end, and place the command \input sshd10.sty in the preamble.

You can easily modify this style file to change the font size or even the font itself. Using the methods described in Section 1.5, for example, you could define bold sans serif commands \Bsfhuge, \BsfLarge, and so on, and replace the following \sf commands by the appropriate bold font.

```
%========================= SSHDBK10.STY ==========================
% SSHDBK10.STY: Makes slightly smaller headings in sans serif font
%               Modified from BK10.STY (changes indicated by ˆˆˆ)
%               Adapted by Dominik Wujastyk
%--------------------------- part --------------------------------
% From book.sty:
\def\@part[#1]#2{\ifnum \c@secnumdepth >-2\relax \refstepcounter{part}
\addcontentsline{toc}{part}{\thepart \hspace{1em}#1}\else
\addcontentsline{toc}{part}{#1}\fi \markboth{}{}
 {\centering \ifnum \c@secnumdepth >-2\relax \Large\sf Part \thepart \par
%                                             ˆˆˆˆˆˆˆˆˆˆ
\vskip 20pt \fi \huge \sf #1\par}\@endpart}
%                  ˆˆˆˆˆˆˆˆˆ
\def\@endpart{\vfil\newpage \if@twoside \hbox{} \thispagestyle{empty}
 \newpage
 \fi \if@tempswa \twocolumn \fi}
\def\@spart#1{{\centering \huge \sf #1\par}\@endpart}
%                          ˆˆˆˆˆˆˆˆˆ
```

```
%------------------------- chapter ------------------------------------
% From bk10.sty:
\def\@makechapterhead#1{ \vspace*{50pt} { \parindent 0pt \raggedright
  \ifnum \c@secnumdepth >\m@ne \huge\sf \@chapapp{} \thechapter \par
  \vskip 20pt \fi \huge \sf #1\par
%                ^^^^^^^^^
  \nobreak \vskip 40pt } }
%
  \def\@makeschapterhead#1{ \vspace*{50pt} { \parindent 0pt \raggedright
  \huge \sf #1\par
%^^^^^^^^^^
  \nobreak \vskip 40pt } }
%
%----------------------- section --------------------------------------
\def\section{\@startsection {section}{1}{\z@}{-3.5ex plus -1ex minus
  -.2ex}{2.3ex plus .2ex}{\Large\sf}}
%                           ^^^
%-------------------- subsection --------------------------------------
\def\subsection{\@startsection{subsection}{2}{\z@}{-3.25ex plus -1ex
  minus -.2ex}{1.5ex plus .2ex}{\large\sf}}
%                             ^^^
%-------------------- subsubsection -----------------------------------
\def\subsubsection{\@startsection{subsubsection}{3}{\z@}{-3.25ex plus
  -1ex minus -.2ex}{1.5ex plus .2ex}{\normalsize\sf}}
%                                   ^^^
%--------------------- paragraph --------------------------------------
\def\paragraph{\@startsection
  {paragraph}{4}{\z@}{3.25ex plus 1ex minus .2ex}{-1em}{\normalsize\sf}}
%                                                 ^^^
%--------------------- subparagraph -----------------------------------
\def\subparagraph{\@startsection
  {subparagraph}{4}{\parindent}{3.25ex plus 1ex minus
  .2ex}{-1em}{\normalsize\sf}}
%               ^^^
%======================================================================
```

9.2.4 Outdenting Headings

Many modern book styles specify that section headings are to be outdented to the
left of the text body. If you want this effect, the `SSBK10.STY` file in the preceding
section can be modified to produce heading outdenting. For example, if you want
the section heading to be outdented to the left by half an inch, the macro for the
`\section` heading in the style file would become

```
%----------------------- section --------------------------------------
%------ modified for outdent of section title
\def\section{\@startsection {section}{1}{\z@}{-3.5ex plus -1ex minus
  -.2ex}{2.3ex plus .2ex}{\leftskip=-2cm \rightskip=0pt plus 1fil \Large\sf}}
%                          ^^^^^^^^^^^^^^^^^^^^^^^^^^^^^^^^^^^^^   ^^^
```

9.2.5   Right Headers to Reference Last Section

The right header normally corresponds to the first section on the page. However, it can be made to refer to the last section. This problem arises only if there is more than one section heading on the same page. Insert in the preamble

```
\makeatletter  \def\rightmark{\expandafter\@rightmark\botmark}  \makeatother
```

9.2.6   New Environment for Indentation of Text

The `indentation` environment defined next allows temporary resetting of the page margins. This environment takes two arguments, which are the left and right indents. The text in between the `\begin{indendation}` and `\end{indendation}` will be set as a paragraph with the specified left and right indentation. Here are some examples.

> This text is set in a centered and right-justified paragraph with larger left and right margins than usual. This paragraph is indented half an inch on each side from the surrounding margins. This was produced with

```
\begin{indentation}{.5in}{.5in}
    This text is set in ...
\end{indentation}
```

These three lines of text are set in a right-justified paragraph that is indented only at the right. The indentation on the right is 1.5 inches, and is produced by `\begin{indentation}{0in}{1.5in}`.

> This text will be indented on the left only by 1 inch from the normal margin with `\begin{indentation}{1.5in}{0in}`.

>> The indentation environment can also be nested, giving indents within indents, as is the text of this paragraph.

> After leaving the second level of indentation, you return to the first indentation level as in this paragraph.

To use this `indentation` environment in your document include the following macro in your preamble (or in your style file after removing the first and last lines):

```
%======================= Indentation Macro ==========================
\makeatletter
\newenvironment{indentation}[2]%
{\par \setlength{\leftmargin}{#1}        \setlength{\rightmargin}{#2}
    \advance\linewidth -\leftmargin     \advance\linewidth -\rightmargin
    \advance\@totalleftmargin\leftmargin \@setpar{{\@@par}}%
    \parshape 1 \@totalleftmargin        \linewidth \ignorespaces}{\par}
\makeatother
%====================================================================
```

9.3   Changing the Caption Format

9.3.1   Changing the Caption Font Size and Width

Frequently, the caption for a figure or table needs to be printed in a smaller font than that used for the main text. Unfortunately, the `\caption` command cannot successfully be embedded in a font size command. Here is a macro for the preamble that can be used to change the font size for the caption, restrict its width, and control the vertical space after the caption.

```
%====================== Macro for small caption =========================
\newlength{\captsize}          \let\captsize=\footnotesize
\newlength{\captwidth}         \setlength{\captwidth}{0.5\textwidth}
\newlength{\beforetableskip}   \setlength{\beforetableskip}{.5\baselineskip}
\newcommand{\capt}[1]{\begin{minipage}{\captwidth}
           \let\normalsize=\captsize
           \caption[#1]{#1}
           \end{minipage}\\ \vspace{\beforetableskip}}
%========================================================================
```

The parameter `\captsize` specifies the font size, `\captwidth` specifies the caption width, and `\beforetableskip` controls the vertical space placed after the caption. Default values are shown in the preceding definition. Table 9.1 is an example of a simple floating table produced with this `\capt` command. It is produced with

```
\begin{table}[htbp]     %--- Table for footnotesize caption
  \centering
    \setlength{\captwidth}{2.0in}
    \capt{The discrete energies $E_i$ (MeV) used for deriving
          the line-beam response function \label{capttst1}}
    \footnotesize   \begin{tabular}{|rc|rc|}
                    ..... (define table)
                  \end{tabular}
\end{table}
```

Table 9.1. The discrete energies E_i (MeV) used for deriving the line-beam response function

i	E_i	i	E_i
1	0.02	6	0.1
2	0.03	7	0.2
3	0.04	8	0.4
4	0.06	9	0.7
5	0.08	10	1.0

9.3.2   Changing the Style of the Caption Label

There is a great variation in how figure and table captions are formatted in different publications. Here is a hack that changes three caption format features: (1) the colon(:) appended to the caption label (for example, "Figure 5.4:" or "Table 10.5:") is replaced by a period(.), (2) the figure or table label is put in boldface, and (3) one-line captions are left justified rather than centered. Place the following in your preamble (or in a style file without the `\makeatletter` and `makeatother`).

```
%=============== Redefine the \@makecaption Command ====================
\makeatletter
        \long\def\@makecaption#1#2{\vskip 10\p@
    %% \setbox\@tempboxa\hbox{#1: #2}%          %% original definition
        \setbox\@tempboxa\hbox{{\bf #1.} #2}%    %% bold and . instead of :
        \ifdim \wd\@tempboxa >\hsize
    %%      #1: #2\par                           %% original definition
            {\bf #1.} #2\par                     %% bold and . instead of :
        \else
    %%      \hbox to\hsize{\hfil\box\@tempboxa\hfil}%   %% original
            \hbox to\hsize{\box\@tempboxa\hfil}%        %% no centering
        \fi}
\makeatother
%======================================================================
```

This macro is easily modified to make other format changes (for example, to have italics labels instead of bold) or to restore some aspect of the default format.

In the following examples, the `\capt` command (see previous subsection) is used instead of the `\caption` command both to restrict the caption width and to use a smaller font. However, the LaTeX `\caption` command also works just as well (although changing font size and width restriction cannot be used). Table 9.2 was produced with the following input.

```
\begin{table}[htbp]
  \begin{center}
    \setlength{\captwidth}{3.0in}
    \capt{A caption in {\protect{\verb|footnotesize|}} font with
        the table label in boldface and the usual colon at the
        end on the label replaced by a period.\label{tab10colon}}
    \framebox[3in]{\rule{0in}{.2in}}
  \end{center}
\end{table}
```

Table 9.2. A caption in `footnotesize` font with the table label in boldface and the usual colon at the end on the label replaced by a period.

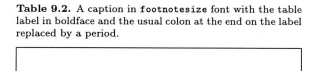

Here is an example of a left-justified label for a one-line caption produced with the redefined `\@makecaption` macro.

Table 9.3. A Short Caption.

9.3.3 Changing *Figure* to *Fig.*

To change the figure label "Figure" to "Fig.", place the following in your preamble (or in a style file without the `\makeatletter` and `\makeatother`).

```
\makeatletter
   \newcommand{\thefigurename}{Figure}   %-- set default: Figure
   \def\fnum@figure{\thefigurename\ \thefigure}
\makeatother
```

Then, to change the figure label from "Figure" to "Fig.", simply redefine the parameter `\thefigurename` by placing the following statement in your document:

```
\renewcommand{\thefigurename}{Fig.}
```

Note: If you place this redefinition inside the `\begin{figure}` ... `\end{figure}`, it will apply only to that figure. Figure 9.1 was produced by the following:

```
\begin{figure}[htbp]
   \begin{center}
   \framebox[3in]{\rule{0in}{.5in}}
   \setlength{\captwidth}{3.0in}
   \renewcommand{\thefigurename}{Fig.}
   \capt{A figure caption in which the figure label has been
         modified to ``Fig.".\label{figfigtest}}
   \end{center}
\end{figure}
```

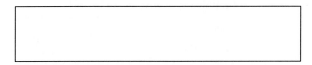

Fig. 9.1. A figure caption in which the figure label has been modified to "Fig.".

9.4   Numbering Things

9.4.1   Page Numbering with "chapter-page"

Here is a style macro that affixes the chapter number by a hyphen to the page number. Moreover, at the beginning of each chapter, the page number is reset to 1.

```
%==================== CHAPPAGE.STY ====================
% Style macros for creating "chapter-page" numbering
%
% Define chapter-page numbering
\renewcommand{\thepage}{\arabic{chapter}-\arabic{page}}
%
% Reset page number when chapter is stepped
\@addtoreset{page}{chapter}
% Reset page counter to one rather than zero
\def\@stpelt#1{\global\csname c@#1\endcsname
          \expandafter\ifx \csname#1\endcsname \page
             \@ne
          \else
          \z@ \fi}
%======================================================
```

Note that if you use any command in your document that changes the macro \thepage, for example, \pagenumbering{roman}, you will have to follow such a command by the \renewcommand... in the above macro.

If you have appendices in the document, then after the \appendix command that starts the appendices, insert the statement

\renewcommand{\thepage}{\Alpha{chapter}-\arabic{page}}

in order to have the appendix pages numbered A-1, A-2, and so on.

9.4.2 Page Numbers to the Right of Text

If the style file `FANCYHDS.STY` is too elaborate for your needs, here is a file that puts the page number 30 points to the right of the right margin. By modifying and playing with it, you can do all sorts of tricks, such as page styles that don't have numbers or that have them centered. This should be put into the document preamble (or into a style file without the `\makeatletter` and `\makeatother` commands).

```
%============== Page Number to Right ==================
\makeatletter          %---- remove if in style file
  \def\ps@right        %---- by Michael Barr
  {\let\@mkboth\markboth
  \def\@oddfoot{}\def\@evenfoot{}
  \def\@evenhead{\rm \thepage\hfil \sl
  \leftmark}\def\@oddhead{\hbox{}\sl \rightmark \hfil
  \hbox to 0pt{\kern30pt \rm\thepage\hss}%
  }\def\sectionmark##1{\markright {\uppercase{
  \ifnum \c@secnumdepth >\z@
     \thesection\hskip 1em\relax \fi ##1}}}}
\makeatother           %---- remove if in style file
%=====================================================
```

9.4.3 Numbering Equations as "(Section.Equation)"

You can obtain equation numbering of the form (*secnum.eqnum*) by including in the document preamble

```
\renewcommand{\theequation}{{\rm
              \thesection.\arabic{equation}}}
```

You must also reset the counter at the beginning of each section with

```
\section{...}    \setcounter{equation}{0}
```

Equivalently, you can add the following to a style file:

```
%-- reset equation number to zero when section begins
     \@addtoreset{equation}{section}
%-- define the equation number style (section.eqn)
     \def\theequation{\thesection.\arabic{equation}}
```

9.5 Equation Tricks

9.5.1 Dashed Lines in Arrays and Tabulars

LaTeX allows only solid horizontal and vertical rules to be placed inside `tabular` or `array` environments. Sometimes it is useful to use dashed lines to show, for example, a partitioned matrix. Nakashima has developed a useful style file `HVDASHLN.STY` (freely available in many TeX Internet archives) that allows horizontal and vertical dashed lines to be placed inside array and tabular environments. Here are some examples.

$$\left(\begin{array}{c:ccc} A_1 & B_1 & 0 & 0 \\ \hdashline C_2 & A_2 & B_2 & 0 \\ 0 & C_3 & A_3 & B_3 \\ 0 & 0 & C_4 & A_4 \end{array} \right)$$

```
\left( \begin{array}{c @{\vdashline}ccc}
    A_1 & B_1 & 0   & 0    \\ \hdashline
    C_2 & A_2 & B_2 & 0    \\
    0   & C_3 & A_3 & B_3  \\
    0   & 0   & C_4 & A_4
    \end{array} \right)
```

a	b	c
a	b	c
a	b	c

```
\begin{tabular}{|c|c|c|} \hline
    a & b & c \\ \hline
    a & b & c \\ \hline
    a & b & c \\ \hline
\end{tabular}
```

a	b	c
a	b	c
a	b	c

```
\begin{tabular}
    {|c @{\vdashline}c|c|} \hdashline
    a & b & c \\ \hdashline
    a & b & c \\ \hline
    a & b & c \\ \hdashline
\end{tabular}
```

The widths of the dashes and the interdash space are set, as in these examples, with

$$\texttt{\textbackslash hdashlinewidth=2pt} \qquad \texttt{\textbackslash hdashlinegap=2pt}$$

9.5.2 Equal Spacing in Equations and Eqnarrays

The spacing around the equal sign in an `eqnarray` environment is larger than that in an `equation` environment. In Section 4.5, a new equation array environment was defined to avoid this problem.

Rather than define a new equation array environment, here is a hack to modify the `eqnarray` environment to give proper spacing around the $=$ sign. Put the following in a style file.

```
%============= eqnarray with proper spacing at = sign ==============
\def\eqnarray{\stepcounter{equation}\let\@currentlabel=\theequation
\global\@eqnswtrue
\global\@eqcnt\z@\tabskip\@centering\let\\=\@eqncr
$$\halign to \displaywidth\bgroup\@eqnsel\hskip\@centering
 $\displaystyle\tabskip\z@{##}$&\global\@eqcnt\@ne
   \hskip 0.28em \hfil${##}$\hfil
   &\global\@eqcnt\tw@ \hskip 0.28em
      $\displaystyle\tabskip\z@{##}$\hfil
      \tabskip\@centering&\llap{##}\tabskip\z@\cr}
%=================================================================
```

9.5.3 Math Macro for Over- and UnderBrackets

Donald Arseneau has written a useful macro \overunderbraces (reproduced here) to put labeled horizontal brackets above and below a mathematical expressions, such as

$$\overbrace{}^{x} \qquad \overbrace{}^{y}$$
$$a + b + \underbrace{c + d + e + f + g + h}_{z} + i + j + k + l + m = \pi r^2 \qquad (9.1)$$

The math command to produce such an expression has the syntax

$\overunderbraces${*upper-brace-spec*}{*main-formula*}{*lower-brace-spec*}

The above example has seven segments shown schematically as follows

```
              x                  y
         ,-----^-----,      ,-----^-----,
  a + b + c + d + e + f + g + h + i + j + k + l + m = \pi r^2
  1111111122222222233333344455555666666667777777777777...
                    '-----v-----'
                          z
```

Then, in composing the math expression, place an **&** between each segment (that is, where the tips of the braces point), as follows:

```
              x                  y
         ,-----^-----,      ,-----^-----,
  a + b +&c + d +&e + f&+&g + h&+ i + j&+ k + l + m
               '-----v-----'
                     z
```

Then each brace is specified by \br{*number-of-segments*}{*label*} separated by &s to indicate the brace's location (with & & indicating a skipped segment). For the preceding example, the upper and lower brace specifiers are

```
top row:     &\br{2}{x}& &\br{2}{y}
bottom row: & &\br{3}{z}
```

Finally, putting this all together, the example of Eq. (9.1) is produced with

```
\begin{equation}
    \overunderbraces{&\br{2}{x}& &\br{2}{y}}%
        {a + b +&c + d +&e + f&+&g + h&+ i + j&+ k + 1 + m}%
        {& &\br{3}{z}} = \pi r^2
\end{equation}
```

Here is the macro, which can be placed in a style file or placed in the document preamble between \makeatletter and \makeatotheer.

```
%================= Over- and Underbraces =====================
% \overunderbraces{upper_braces}{main_formula}{lower_braces}
% by D. Arseneau
\def\overunderbraces #1#2#3{{%
  \baselineskip\z@skip \lineskip4\p@ \lineskiplimit4\p@
  \displaystyle   %% generate error if not in math mode!
%first, do top half of the alignment ina save-box ...
  \setbox\z@\vbox{\ialign{&\hfil$\{}##{}$\hfil\cr
    \global\let\br\br@label #1\cr  %upper labels
    \global\let\br\br@down #1\cr   %upper braces
    #2\cr % main line of the formula
  }}% finished partial alignment and \vbox.
  \dimen@-\ht\z@ %   Measure height of partial alignment --
%... it is the height we want for the whole.
% Now do the whole alignment (notice the repetition from above)
  \setbox\z@\vbox{\ialign{&\hfil$\{}##{}$\hfil\cr
    \global\let\br\br@label #1\cr  %upper labels
    \global\let\br\br@down #1\cr   %upper braces
    #2\cr    %main line of the formula
    \global\let\br\br@up #3\cr      %lower braces
    \global\let\br\br@label #3\cr  %lower labels
  }}% finished whole alignment and \vbox.
  \advance\dimen@\ht\z@ %calc. the necessary lowering
  \lower\dimen@\hbox{\box\z@} % shift to get the desired height
}}
% Three aliases for \br  #1=number of spanned columns, #2=label
\def\br@up#1#2{\multispan{#1}\upbracefill}
\def\br@down#1#2{\multispan{#1}\downbracefill}
\def\br@label#1#2{\multispan{#1}\hidewidth $#2$\hidewidth}
%============================================================
```

9.6   References, Bibliographies, and Endnotes

9.6.1   Superscripts for References

To make reference citations appear as superscipts [5] rather than the default [5] used
by LaTeX, you need to change the macro `\@cite` that defines their appeerence. Add
the following to your style file:

```
%==================== RAISEDCITE.STY =================
% Produces superscript references: by Terry Anderson
\newif\ifraisedcite
\def\raisedcitations{\raisedcitetrue}
\def\noraisedcitations{\raisedcitefalse}
\raisedcitations% default
\def\@cite#1#2{%
    \ifraisedcite\raisebox{.8ex}
       {\scriptsize [{#1\if@tempswa , #2\fi}]}   %<<<
    \else [{#1\if@tempswa , #2\fi}]\fi}
%====================================================
```

In this style, if `\raisedcitations` is declared, the citations are raised above the
lines like footnotes. The `\noraisedcitations` command causes the normal citation
style to be used. To eliminate the [and] in the raised style, simply delete the [
and] in the line flagged by `%<<<`. Likewise, you could replace the square brackets
by parentheses or omit any delimiters at all.

9.6.2   Line Breaks for Long Citations

LaTeX does not break citations and long ones such as [Kwiatkowska et al., 1990]
can give overfilled lines very easily. To allow LaTeX to break a citation across a line,
the `/@citex` command in `LATEX.TEX` must be modified. Specifically, change the
definition of `\@citex` in `LATEX.TEX` by removing just the `\hbox` and *nothing* else.
You will then need to put in ties (~) wherever you do not want a citation broken at
the end of a line.

9.6.3   Bibliographies at Chapter Ends

For some reports or books, a separate bibliography may be desired at the end of each
chapter. In such a style, the citations in each chapter are to be independent of those
in other chapters. Unfortunately, LaTeX allows only a single bibliography for each
document. There is a style `CHAPTERBIB.STY`, freely available from many Internet
TeX archives, that allows each chapter to have its own independent bibliography.

As an altertnative, here is a smaller and more limited style file that can be used if you put each chapter into a separate file and then \include each file into the root document (see Section 7.1). At the end of each chapter's file, you put a \begin{thebibliography} ... \end{thebibliography} block containing all the references for the chapter to force the chapter bibliography to be printed.

```
%======================= BIBPERINCLUDE.STY =====================
\def\@mainbblfile{\jobname.bbl}
\let\@bblfile=\@mainbblfile
\def\bibliography#1{\if@filesw
   \immediate\write\@auxout{\string\bibdata{#1}}\fi
\@input{\@bblfile}}
\def\@include#1 {\clearpage
   \if@filesw \immediate\write\@mainaux{\string\@input{#1.aux}}\fi
   \@tempswatrue
   \if@partsw
      \@tempswafalse   \edef\@tempb{#1}%
      \@for \@tempa:=\@partlist \do{%
         \ifx \@tempa\@tempb \@tempswatrue \fi }\fi
   \if@tempswa
      \if@filesw
         \let\@auxout\@partaux
         \immediate\openout\@partaux #1.aux
         \immediate\write\@partaux{\relax}\fi
      \def\@bblfile{#1.bbl}\@input{#1.tex}\clearpage
      \let\@bblfile\@mainbblfile
      \@writeckpt{#1}%
      \if@filesw
         \immediate\closeout\@partaux
      \fi
      \let\@auxout\@mainaux
      \else
         \@nameuse{cp@#1}%
      \fi }
\endinput
%================================================================
```

9.6.4 Macro for Endnotes

For short documents, you may want to use endnotes rather than footnotes. Here is a style file that is a minor modification of a similar one by Erica Harris that produces endnotes.

Use \endnote{*endnotetext*} to generate the reference number in the text just as you would with \footnote. At the end of your document (or at the end of each chapter), type \producenotes to output all endnotes created since the beginning of the document or since the last \producenotes. The following style file produces the endnotes in \footnotesize using the default font. The fifth line from the bottom (marked by %<<<) can be modified to change the font and its size.

```
%%======================= ENDNOTES.STY ============================
%% AUTHOR: Erica M. S. Harris (modified by JKS)
\newbox\endnotebox
\newcounter{endnotecount}
\def\endnote{\stepcounter{endnotecount}%
        \xdef\@theenmark{\theendnotecount}\@endnotemark\@endnotetext}
\def\@endnotemark{\leavevmode\ifhmode\edef\@x@sf{\the\spacefactor}\fi%
                \hbox{$^{\@theenmark}$}%
        \ifhmode\spacefactor\@x@sf\fi\relax}
\long\def\@endnotetext#1{\global\setbox\endnotebox=
   \vbox{\hsize\columnwidth\@parboxrestore
   \def\baselinestretch{1}\@normalsize
   \unvbox\endnotebox\@makeentext{\ignorespaces#1\strut\par}}}
\long\def\@makeentext#1{\parindent 1em \noindent
% \hbox to 1.8em{\hss\@theenmark.~}#1}   %%-- use for normalsize
   \hbox to 1.8em{\hss\footnotesize\@theenmark.~}\footnotesize#1} %<<<
\def\producenotes{%
\ifvoid\endnotebox\else\medskip\unvbox\endnotebox\par\fi%
\setcounter{endnotecount}{0}}
%%==================================================================
```

Appendix A

Symbols Available in Math Mode

Greek Letters

α	\alpha	θ	\theta	o	o	τ	\tau
β	\beta	ϑ	\vartheta	π	\pi	υ	\upsilon
γ	\gamma	ι	\iota	ϖ	\varpi	ϕ	\phi
δ	\delta	κ	\kappa	ρ	\rho	φ	\varphi
ϵ	\epsilon	λ	\lambda	ϱ	\varrho	χ	\chi
ε	\varepsilon	μ	\mu	σ	\sigma	ψ	\psi
ζ	\zeta	ν	\nu	ς	\varsigma	ω	\omega
η	\eta	ξ	\xi				
Γ	\Gamma	Λ	\Lambda	Σ	\Sigma	Ψ	\Psi
Δ	\Delta	Ξ	\Xi	Υ	\Upsilon	Ω	\Omega
Θ	\Theta	Π	\Pi	Φ	\Phi		

Binary Operation Symbols

$\pm$	\pm	$\cap$	\cap	$\diamond$	\diamond	$\oplus$	\oplus
$\mp$	\mp	$\cup$	\cup	$\triangle$	\bigtriangleup	$\ominus$	\ominus
$\times$	\times	$\uplus$	\uplus	$\triangledown$	\bigtriangledown	$\otimes$	\otimes
$\div$	\div	$\sqcap$	\sqcap	$\triangleleft$	\triangleleft	$\oslash$	\oslash
$\ast$	\ast	$\sqcup$	\sqcup	$\triangleright$	\triangleright	$\odot$	\odot
$\star$	\star	$\vee$	\vee	$\lhd$	\lhd	$\bigcirc$	\bigcirc
$\circ$	\circ	$\wedge$	\wedge	$\rhd$	\rhd	$\dagger$	\dagger
$\bullet$	\bullet	$\setminus$	\setminus	$\unlhd$	\unlhd	$\ddagger$	\ddagger
$\cdot$	\cdot	$\wr$	\wr	$\unrhd$	\unrhd	$\amalg$	\amalg

Relation Symbols

$\leq$	\leq	$\geq$	\geq	$\equiv$	\equiv	$\models$	\models
$\prec$	\prec	$\succ$	\succ	$\sim$	\sim	$\perp$	\perp
$\preceq$	\preceq	$\succeq$	\succeq	$\simeq$	\simeq	$\mid$	\mid
$\ll$	\ll	$\gg$	\gg	$\asymp$	\asymp	$\parallel$	\parallel
$\subset$	\subset	$\supset$	\supset	$\approx$	\approx	$\bowtie$	\bowtie
$\subseteq$	\subseteq	$\supseteq$	\supseteq	$\cong$	\cong	$\Join$	\Join
$\sqsubset$	\sqsubset	$\sqsupset$	\sqsupset	$\neq$	\neq	$\smile$	\smile
$\sqsubseteq$	\sqsubseteq	$\sqsupseteq$	\sqsupseteq	$\doteq$	\doteq	$\frown$	\frown
$\vdash$	\vdash	$\dashv$	\dashv				

Math-mode Accents

$\hat{p}$	\hat{p}	$\acute{p}$	\acute{p}	$\bar{p}$	\bar{p}	$\dot{p}$	\dot{p}
$\check{p}$	\check{p}	$\grave{p}$	\grave{p}	$\vec{p}$	\vec{p}	$\ddot{p}$	\ddot{p}
$\breve{p}$	\breve{p}	$\tilde{p}$	\tilde{p}				

Miscellaneous Symbols

ℵ	`\aleph`	′	`\prime`	∀	`\forall`	∞	`\infty`
ℏ	`\hbar`	∅	`\emptyset`	∃	`\exists`	□	`\Box`
ι	`\imath`	∇	`\nabla`	¬	`\neg`	◇	`\Diamond`
ȷ	`\jmath`	√	`\surd`	♭	`\flat`	△	`\triangle`
ℓ	`\ell`	⊤	`\top`	♮	`\natural`	♣	`\clubsuit`
℘	`\wp`	⊥	`\bot`	♯	`\sharp`	◇	`\diamondsuit`
ℜ	`\Re`	‖	`\	—`	\	`\backslash`	♡	`\heartsuit`
ℑ	`\Im`	∠	`\angle`	∂	`\partial`	♠	`\spadesuit`

Arrow Symbols

←	`\leftarrow`	⟵	`\longleftarrow`	↑	`\uparrow`
⇐	`\Leftarrow`	⟸	`\Longleftarrow`	⇑	`\Uparrow`
→	`\rightarrow`	⟶	`\longrightarrow`	↓	`\downarrow`
⇒	`\Rightarrow`	⟹	`\Longrightarrow`	⇓	`\Downarrow`
↔	`\leftrightarrow`	⟷	`\longleftrightarrow`	↕	`\updownarrow`
⇔	`\Leftrightarrow`	⟺	`\Longleftrightarrow`	⇕	`\Updownarrow`
↦	`\mapsto`	⟼	`\longmapsto`	↗	`\nearrow`
↩	`\hookleftarrow`	↪	`\hookrightarrow`	↘	`\searrow`
↼	`\leftharpoonup`	⇀	`\rightharpoonup`	↙	`\swarrow`
↽	`\leftharpoondown`	⇁	`\rightharpoondown`	↖	`\nwarrow`

Special Functions

arccos	`\arccos`	cos	`\cos`	csc	`\csc`	exp	`\exp`
ker	`\ker`	lim sup	`\limsup`	min	`\min`	sinh	`\sinh`
arcsin	`\arcsin`	cosh	`\cosh`	deg	`\deg`	gcd	`\gcd`
lg	`\lg`	ln	`\ln`	Pr	`\Pr`	sup	`\sup`
arctan	`\arctan`	cot	`\cot`	det	`\det`	hom	`\hom`
lim	`\lim`	log	`\log`	sec	`\sec`	tan	`\tan`
arg	`\arg`	coth	`\coth`	dim	`\dim`	inf	`\inf`
lim inf	`\liminf`	max	`\max`	sin	`\sin`	tanh	`\tanh`

Delimiters

(	`(`	)	`)`	[	`[`	]	`]`
{	`\{`	}	`\}`	⌊	`\lfloor`	⌋	`\rfloor`
⌈	`\lceil`	⌉	`\rceil`	⟨	`\langle`	⟩	`\rangle`
/	`/`	\	`\backslash`	|	—	‖	`\	—`
↑	`\uparrow`	↓	`\downarrow`	⇑	`\Uparrow`	⇓	`\Downarrow`
↕	`\updownarrow`	⇕	`\Updownarrow`				

Appendix B

Format Parameters

In this appendix, many of the parameters that determine how your document is formatted are described. To change the default value of a length parameter, you can use LaTeX's `\setlength` command. For example, to change the indentation for a paragraph to 2 cm, you would use

> `\setlength{\parindent}{2cm}`

Some format parameters define a fractional quantity or a scale factor. To change these parameters, use the `\renewcommand`. For example, to change the fraction of a page that can be occupied by floats at the top use

> `\renewcommand{\topfraction}{.4}`

Finally, some parameters are counters with integer values. Change these counters with the `\setcounter` command. For example, to change the maximum number of floats allowed at the top of a page to three use

> `\setcounter{topnumber}{3}`

Some parameters can be changed only in the preamble. Unless noted to the contrary in the following definitions, a parameter may be changed anywhere in the document.

Page Format Parameters

\oddsidemargin The left indentation of the text relative to one inch from the left margin of the paper. If a `twoside` document style is specified, it only affects odd-numbered pages. *Change in preamble only.* Default values: report, 0.29in (2-sided) or 0.55in (1-sided); book, 0.25in; article, 0.29in (2-sided) or 0.55in (1-sided); letter, 0.74in. Change with the \setlength command.

\evensidemargin In `twoside` style, the left indentation of the text relative to one inch from the left margin of the paper fort even pages. *Change in preamble only.* Default values: report, 0.82in (2-sided) or 0.55in (1-sided); book, 1.25in; article, 0.82in (2-sided) or 0.55in (1-sided); letter, 0.74in. Change with the \setlength command.

\textwidth The text width between the left and right margins in a normal paragraph. *Change only in the preamble.* Default: report, 5.42in; book, 5in; article, 5.42in; letter, 5.07in. Change with the \setlength command.

\topmargin The distance between the top of the paper and the top of the page head. *Change only in the preamble.* Default: 0.38in (book, 0.73in). Change with the \setlength command.

\headheight The vertical space used for a page's header. *Change only in preamble.* Default: 0.17in. Change with the \setlength command.

\headsep The vertical distance between the header and the body of the text. *Change only in the preamble.* Default: report, 0.35in; book, 0.275in; article, 0.35in; letter, 0.63in. Change with the \setlength command.

\textheight Height of the body of the text on a page. *Change only in preamble.* Default: 7.39in (letter, 7.01in). Change with the \setlength command.

\footheight The height of the footer. *Change only in the preamble.* Default: 0in (letter, 0.17in). Change with the \setlength command.

\footskip The distance from the bottom of the text body to the *bottom* of the footer. *Change only in the footer.* Default: 0.42in (letter, 0.35in). Change with the \setlength command.

\parindent Indentation from the left margin for the first line of a paragraph. Default: 1.5em (letter, 0in). Change with the \setlength command.

\baselineskip The minimum separation between baselines in a paragraph. (Letters without descenders are placed on the baseline.) Only one setting per paragraph is allowed. Default: 0.2in (letter, 0.21in). Change with the \setlength command.

`\topskip` Distance from the top of the text body to the baseline of the first line in the body. *Change only in the preamble.* Default: 0.14in. Change with the `\setlength` command.

`\baselinestretch` The space between baselines is multiplied by this factor. Default: 1. Change with the `\renewcommand`. If changed in the document, it does not take effect until after a change in font size. Change with the `\renewcommand` command.

`\parskip` The vertical separation between paragraphs. *This is a rubber length.* Default: 0in (letter, 0.1in). Change with the `\setlength` command.

Section-level Parameters

`secnumdepth` A counter whose value defines the lowest level of sectional numbering. *Set only in preamble.* For report and book styles, chapters are level 0 and parts are level -1. Sections are level 1, subsections level 2, subsubsections level 3, and so on. Change with the `\setcounter` command.

`tocdepth` A counter that defines the lowest level of sections to be included in the Table of Contents. *Set only in preamble.* Change with the `\setcounter` command.

Footnote Parameter

`\footnotesep` The extra separation between footnotes. Default: 0.12in (letter, 0.17in). Change with the `\setlength` command.

Two-column Format Parameters

`\columnsep` The separation between the two columns. Default: 0.14in. Change with the `\setlength` command.

`\columnseprule` The width of the rule placed between columns. If set to 0 size, then no rule is made. Default: 0in. Change with the `\setlength` command.

Marginal Note Parameters

\marginparwidth Width for the marginal notes. *Change only in the preamble.* Default: report and article, 1.18in (two-sided printing) or 0.94in (one-sided printing); book, 1.0in; letter, 1.25in. Change with the **\setlength** command.

\marginparsep The distance between the edge of the text body and the marginal note. *Change only in the preamble.* Default: report and article, 0.14in; book, 0.10in; letter, 0.15in. Change with the **\setlength** command.

\marginparpush The minimum vertical distance between adjacent marginal notes. *Change only in the preamble.* Default: report, book, and article, 0.1in; letter, 0.070in. Change with the **\setlength** command.

List Parameters

All the parameters for the **list** environment are changed in the list environment. For example, you might have

> ...\begin{list}{}{\listparindent .25in \leftmargin .5in}...

\topsep Vertical space (in addition to normal paragraph spacing) between the list and surrounding text. *It is a rubber length.* Default: 0.125in (letter, 0.4em).

\partopsep Extra vertical space between list and surrounding text if a blank line precedes the text. *It is a rubber length.*

\itemsep Separation (added to **\parsep**) between list items. *It is a rubber length.* Default: 0.06in (letter, 0.4em).

\parsep Vertical spacing between paragraphs within an item. *It is a rubber length.* Default: 0.06in (letter, 0in).

\leftmargin The left margin of an item's text (not including the label) relative to the left margin of the text. It must be positive or zero. Default: 2.5em.

\rightmargin The right margin of an item's text (not including the label) relative to the right margin of the text. It must be positive or zero. Default: 0em.

\listparindent The paragraph indentation for all item paragraphs (except the first). Default: 0in.

\itemindent The indentation before each label. Default: 0in (may be negative!).

`\labelsep`   The horizontal separation between a item's label and the text of the item. Default: 0.5em.

`\labelwidth`   The width of the box for each item's label in which the label is placed flush left. If the width of the label's box plus `\labelsep` equals `\leftmargin`, then the label will be flush with the left margin of the surrounding text. If the width of the label's box plus the `\labelsep` is less than the `\leftmargin`, then the labels will be indented from the surrounding text. Default: 2em.

Math Parameters

`\jot`   The extra vertical space added between rows of lines in an `eqnarray` environment. Default: 0.04in. Change with the `\setlength` command.

`\mathindent`   The amount by which the displayed equations are indented from the left margin when `fleqn` document style is specified. Default: 0in. Change with the `\setlength` command.

`\abovedisplayskip`   The extra vertical space left above a long displayed equation (equal to `\topsep` if `fleqn` is used). An equation is considered a long equation if its left end is farther to the left than the end of the last line of text. Default: 0.17in. Change with the `\setlength` command.

`\belowdisplayskip`   The extra vertical space placed below a long displayed equation (equal to `\topsep` if `fleqn` is used). *It is a rubber length.* Default: 0in. Change with the `\setlength` command.

`\abovedisplayshortskip`   The extra vertical space left above a short displayed equation (equal to `\topsep` if `fleqn` is used). An equation is considered a short equation if its left end is farther to the right than the end of the last line of text. Default: 0in. Change with the `\setlength` command.

`\belowdisplayshortskip`   The extra vertical space placed below a short displayed equation (equal to `\topsep` if `fleqn` is used). *It is a rubber length.* Default: 0in. Change with the `\setlength` command.

Float Parameters

`topnumber`   A counter specifying the maximum number of floats that may appear at the top of a text page. Default: 2. Change with the `\setcounter` command.

\topfraction The fraction of a page allowed for floats at the top of the page. Default: 0.7. The \renewcommand is used to change its value.

bottomnumber A counter specifying the maximum number of floats that may appear at the bottom of a text page. Default: 1. Change with the \setcounter command.

\bottomfraction The fraction of a page allowed for floats at the bottom of the page. Default: 0.3. The \renewcommand is used to change its value.

totalnumber A counter specifying the maximum number of floats that may appear on a page (in any position). Default: 3. Change with the \setcounter command.

\textfraction The fraction of any page with floats *and* text that must be occupied with text. Default: 0.2. The \renewcommand is used to change its value.

\floatpagefraction The fraction of a page that must be occupied with floats. The rest of the page may be occupied with floats or white space. Default: 0.5. The \renewcommand is used to change its value.

dbltopnumber A counter specifying the maximum number of double-column floats that may appear at the top of a column in two-column format. Default: 2. Change with the \setcounter command.

\dbltopfraction The fraction of a page allowed for floats at the top of a column in two-column format. Default: 0.7. The \renewcommand is used to change its value.

\dblfloatpagefraction The fraction of a column that must be occupied with floats in two-column format. The rest of the column may be occupied with floats or white space. Default: 0.5. The \renewcommand is used to change its value.

\floatsep The separation between adjacent floats on a text page. *It is a rubber length.* Default: 0.19in (letter, 0.17in).

\textfloatsep The separation between floats and adjacent text. *It is a rubber length.* Default: 0.28in. Change with the \setlength command.

\intextsep The vertical space between floats in the middle of a page and the surrounding text. *This is a rubber length.* Default: 0.19in (letter, 0.17in). Change with the \setlength command.

\dblfloatsep The separation between adjacent floats on a text page in two-column format. *It is a rubber length.* Default: 0.19in (letter, 0.17in). Change with the \setlength command.

\dbltextfloatsep   The separation between floats and the adjacent text in two-column format. *It is a rubber length.* Default: 0.28in. Change with the \setlength command.

Tabular and Array Parameters

\tabcolsep   The width of the blank space at the right and left of each **tabular** column. The space between adjacent columns is twice this value. Default: 0.08in. Change with the \setlength command.

\arraycolsep   The width of the blank space at the right and left of each **array** column. The space between adjacent columns is twice this value. Default: 0.07in. Change with the \setlength command.

\arrayrulewidth   The width of the vertical rule | in a **tabular** or **array** environment. It is also the width of the horizontal lines produced with \hline and \cline. Default: 0.006in. Change with the \setlength command.

\doublerulesep   The separation between double rule lines in **tabular** or **array** environments produced with the || command or two successive \hline or \cline commands. Default: 0.03in. Change with the \setlength command.

\arraystretch   The normal spacing between successive lines in the **tabular** or **array** environments is multiplied by this value. Default: 1. This value is changed with the **renewcommand**.

Box Parameters

\fboxrule   The width of the lines produced by a \fbox or \framebox command. (It does not affect \framebox within the **picture** environment.) Default: 0.006in. Change with the \setlength command.

\fboxsep   The distance between the rule of a box and its contents produced by the \fbox and \framebox commands. (It does not affect \framebox within the **picture** environment.) Default: 0.04in. Change with the \setlength command.

Index

␣ space symbol, 29
\␣ full space, 11, 46
~ lock space, 12
& `tabular` column separator, 65
\! negative space, 46, 52
\' `tabbing` left shift, 62
\+ `tabbing` left margin indent , 62
\, thin space, 11, 46
\- `tabbing` left outdent, 62
\/ italics space correction, 11
\: medium math space, 46
\< `tabbing` outdent, 62
\= `tabbing` set tab, 62
\> `tabbing` next tab, 62
\@ inter sentence spacing, 11
\\ line break, 12, 47-48, 62, 65
\' `tabbing` flush right margin, 62

\abovedisplayshortskip, 167
\abovedisplayskip, 167
accents
    math, 43, 160
    text, 1
\addcontentsline, 111
\addtocounter, 35, 36
adding space
    in text mode, 11, 17-18,
    in math mode, 46
aligning
    decimals in tables, 67
    table headings, 67
    vertically in tables, 72
$\mathcal{AMS}$-LaTeX , 10, 42
arabic page numbering, 111
array, 55-56
    font size, 51-52
    formatting, 169

partitioned, 152
\arraycolsep, 48, 169
\arrayrulewidth, 74, 169
\arraystretch, 74, 169
arrow symbols, 161
arrows, 85
assignment statement, 141

backslash, 1
\baselineskip, 31, 40, 164
\baselinestretch, 12-13, 165
\begingroup, 142
\begin{document}, 105
\begin{thebibliography}, 114
\begin{theindex}, 117
\belowdisplayshortskip, 167
\belowdisplayskip, 167
bezier spline, 86
\bezier, 86
\bf, 2
\bgroup, 142
\bibitem, 115
bibliography, 114-115, 114-116
    as endnotes, 155-156
    at chapter ends, 155
    example, 119
    printing, 115
binary operators, 160
binomials, example, 43
blank pages, 35
boldface
    in math mode, 53
    in text mode, 2
\boldmath, 2, 53-54
\bottomfraction, 37, 38-39, 168
bottomnumber, 38, 168
boxes, 18-21, 57-59, 73

centering, 21
fancy, 133-134
formatting, 169
in `picture`, 84
large, 134
right justify, 19
saving, 88
with frame, 18-19
with footnotes, 113
braces
  horizontal, 153
  over and under, 153
break
  line, 12, 14, 16
  page, 35

`\cal`, 2
calligraphic, 2
`\caption`, 61, 68, 115
captions
  changing format, 147
  Fig. label, 149
  hanging indent, 122
  label style, 148
  width restriction, 68
  width, 147
`\captionwidth`, 123
`\centerpcl`, 94
cents symbol, 9
`\chapter`, 16
chemical reactions, 52-53, 57
`\choose`, 43
`\circle`, 85
citations, 114-115, 116
  format, 115
  in captions, 115
  in tables, 116
  line break, 155
  with superscripts, 155
`\cite`, 115
`\cleardoublepage`, 41
`\clearpage`, 35
`\clearpage`, 41
`\cline`, 65
`\clubpenalty`, 35
column breaking, 41

`\columnsep`, 40, 165
`\columnseprule`, 40, 165
commands
  assignment, 141
  conditionals, 141
  creating, 139-140
  defining, 139-140
  internal, 140
  looping, 141-142
computer modern font, 2, 3
continued fractions, 56-57
counters, 36
  for `enumerate` list, 23
  user defined, 36
cross references, 113-114
CTAN, 120

`\dashbox`, 84
`\dblfloatpagefraction`, 168
`\dblfloatsep`, 168
`\dbltextfloatsep`, 169
`\dbltopfraction`, 168
`dbltopnumber`, 168
`\def`, 140
defining commands, 139-140
defining counters, 36
defining environment, 26
delimiters, 161
`description` environment, 24
displaymath, 42
`\displaystyle`, 50
document
  large, 105-119
  styles, 108
    `article`, 139
    bezier, 86
    `book`, 139
    `letter`, 139
    non-standard, 120-137
    `report`, 139
    two-column, 39-41
`\documentstyle`, 107
`\dotfill`, 18
double space, 12-13
`\doublerulesep`, 74, 169
drawing pictures, 81-88

DVIPS, 98-99

\egroup, 142
\em, 2
emTEX, 92
\endgroup, 142
endnotes, 155
\end{document}, 105
\end{thebibliography}, 114
\end{theindex}, 117
end of line, 12, 47-48, 62, 65, 155
enumerate environment, 23
environments,
  array, 50-51, 55-56
  eqnarray, 50-51
  flushleft, 15
  description, 24
  enumerate, 23
  eqnarray, 47-48
  figure*, 41
  figure, 37
  figwindow, 127
  itemize, 21-22
  list, 24
  minipage, 18
  picture, 81, 83-88
  tabbing, 61-64
  table*, 41
  table, 37
  tabular, 64-75
  tabwindow, 127
  text indentation, 146
  thebibliography, 114
  theindex, 117
  verbatim, 28-29
  window, 127
  wrapfigure, 126
EPIC, 81, 89
EPSF macros, 99-100
\epsfbox, 100
\epsffile, 100
eqalign, 124
eqalignno, 124
eqaligntwo, 125
eqnarray, (see also *environment*)
  font size, 51-52

spacing in, 48, 51-52
text in, 48
\eqno, 51
EQUATION.STY, 123-125
equations, 42-59
  aligned, 124
  chemical, 52-53, 57
  flexible numbering, 123-125
  framed, 57-59
  left and right tags, 51
  multi-conditional, 47
  multi-line, 47
  numbering, 42, 51, 151
  simple, 46
  subequations, 125
  two aligned, 125
  with struts, 49
  cases, 125
\evensidemargin, 30, 31, 40, 164
\everymath, 53
excluding input, 112
\exhyphenpenalty, 14

face, type, 2, 4
FANCYBOX.STY, 133-134
FANCYHDS.STY, 34, 129-132
\fbox, 18-19
\fboxrule, 19, 169
\fboxsep, 19, 169
\fi, 141
figures
  floating, 94-96
  importing, 82-82, 92-102
  incorporating, 80-104
  positioning, 36-39
  wrapped by text, 126-128
\fill, 17
\floatpagefraction, 38-39, 168
floats, 36-39
  graphics, 81
  number on page, 38
  piling up of, 38
  positioning, 37
  positioning, 167-168
  two-column, 41
\floatsep, 37, 168

`flushleft`, 15
`\fnsymbol`, 113
`\font`, specifying character, 6
fonts
    availability, 4-5
    blackboard, 9
    changing in headings, 145
    computer modern, 3
    faces, 4
    improvised, 9-10, 54-55
    load on demand, 5
    math italics, 52
    math mode, 7
    NFSS, 10
    non-standard, 6
    one inch, 7
    scaling, 3-4
    sizes
      text mode, 2
      math mode, 50
    smiley faces, 9-10
    styles, 2
footers, 32-34
    customized, 129-132
`\footheight`, 30, 31, 40, 164
`\footnote`, 13, 112-113
footnote, 112
    in boxes, 113
    in heading, 112-113
    symbols, 113
`\footnotemark`, 113
`\footnotesep`, 165
`\footnotesize`, 2
`\footnotetext`, 113
`\footskip`, 30, 31, 31, 40, 40, 164
format parameters, 163-169
formatting
    arrays, 169
    boxes, 169
    floats, 165-166
    footnote, 164
    lists, 164
    margin notes, 164
    math, 165
    pages, 164-165
    tables, 169

two columns, 164-165
formulas (see equations)
`\frac`, 43
fractions, 50
    continued, 56-57
    examples, 43
`\frame`, 86-87
`\framebox`, 18-19, 57-59, 84
frames, 57-59
    fancy, 133-134
    large, 134
front matter, 108-112
    page numbering, 111
frown, 9
function symbols, 161
`\fussy`, 12

`\global`, 140
GNUPLOT, 90-91
graphics
    GNUPLOT, 90-91
    approaches, 80-83
    beside text, 95
    bit-mapped files, 92-98
    conversion, 103-104
    cut and paste, 80
    EPIC, 81, 89
    floats, 81
    from other programs, 90
    importing, 82-83
    in paragraphs, 97
    non-LaTeX, 92-104///
    PCL files, 82-83
    positioning, 93-98
    PostScript
      example, 102
      files, 98-104
      using, 82-83
    side-by-side, 96
    `\special` command, 83
    PiCTeX, 82, 89
    `picture`, 81
    TeXCAD, 82
    xfig, 82
greek letters, 160
growing symbols, examples, 44

HANGCAPTION.STY, 122-123
\hangcaption, 96, 122-123
hanging indents, 20
headers, 32-34
    customized, 129-132
    for last section, 146
\headheight, 30, 31, 40, 164
headings, 16
    fonts for, 144
    line break, 16
    numbering, 16
    outdenting, 145
    suppressing numbering, 16
    with math, 59
\headsep, 30, 31, 40, 164
\hfill, 17-18
HiJack, 103
\hline, 65
HP2xx, 103
HPGL graphics, 82-83, 103
\hrulefill, 18
\hspace, 17
\Huge, 2
\huge, 2
HVDASHLN.STY/, 152
hyphen.tex, 139
\hyphenation, 14
hyphenation, 13-14
    at line break, 14
    forcing, 14
    preventing at line break, 14
    turning off, 14
    with ragged right, 15
\hyphenpenalty, 14

\if, 141
\ifthenelse, 141, 141
importing graphics, 92-184
    PCL files, 92-98
    PostScript, 98-104
\include, 106
\includeonly, 105
indentation, 20, 146
\index, 116
index, making, 116-118
\indexspace, 117

\input, 82, 107
\int, 45
intercolumn space, 40, 165
itemize environment, 21-22
Internet, 120-121, 138
\intextsep, 37, 168
\it, 2
italics typestyle, 2-3, 52
\item, 22-17
\itemindent, 166
itemize environment, 21-23
\itemsep, 166

\jot, 167
justification, line, 15

\kill, 62

\label, 46, 114
\labelsep, 167
\labelwidth, 167
\Large, 2
\LARGE, 2
\large, 2
LaTeX archives, 121
\left, 49
\leftmargin, 166
\leftmark, 34
\let, 141
lfonts.tex, 139
ligatures, 5
line break, 12
    at hyphen, 14
    in heading, 16
line justification, 15
line spacing, 12-13, 12-13
    in footnotes, 13
\line, 85
lines, 85
    in arrays, 152
\list, format parameters, 25
\listoffigures, 110
\listoftables, 110
\listparindent, 166
lists, 21-27
    aligned, 27-28
    contents, 109-112

customized, 24-26
description, 24
enumerate, 23
figures, 110
for references, 27
formatting, 166-167
itemize, 21-22
   symbols for, 22
   two columns, 22
tables, 110
verbatim, 121
`\load`, 5
load-on-demand fonts, 5
lock space, 12
`lof`, 110-111
logical switches, 141
`\long\def`, 140
looping, 141-142
`lot`, 110-111
lowering text, 18-19
`lplain.tex`, 139

macros
   assignment statement, 141
   basics, 139-142
   bibliography per chapter, 155
   conditional statement, 141
   endnotes, 155
   equation numbering, 151
   for captions, 147-149
   for heading font, 145
   grouping, 142
   in preamble, 107-108
   looping, 142
   new command, 139-141
   over and under braces, 153
   page numbering, 150
   side-by-side displays, 142-143
   spacing in **eqnarray**, 152
   striking out, 143
   text indentation, 146
   underlining, 143
`\magstep`, 3-4
`\makeatletter`, 15, 34, 108, 140-141
`\makeatother`, 15, 34, 108, 140-141
`\makebox`, 18-19, 84, 86-87

`makeidx`, 118
`\makeindex`, 116
MAKEINDEX, 118
margin note, 32, 41
   formatting, 166
margins, document, 30-31
`\marginpar`, 32, 41
`\marginparpush`, 32, 166
`\marginparsep`, 32, 166
`\marginparwidth`, 32, 166
`\markboth`, 32-33
`\markright`, 32-33
math modes, 42
math
   accents, 54, 160
      examples, 43
   boldface, 53
   compound operators, 55
   continued fractions, 56-57
   delimiters, 161, 161
   examples, 43-45
   font sizes, 50
   formatting, 167
   functions, 161
   in section titles, 59
   italics, 2, 52
   multi-letter variables, 52
   roman font, 52-53
   same size delimiters, 49
   spacing, 46
   struts in, 49
   symbols, 160-161
`\mathindent`, 167
matrices, 55-56
   examples, 44
   partitioned, 152
`\mbox`, 7, 14, 47
metafont, 9
micro spacing, 11
`minipage`, 18
   for tables, 69-73
`minipage`, for graphics, 95-96
multi-column text, 135-137
MULTICOLS.STY, 135-137
`\multicolumn`, 65
`\multiput`, 87

\newcommand, 52, 107, 139
\newcounter, 26, 28
\newenvironment, 26-28, 107
\newfont, 3, 6
\newline, 12
\newpage, 41
\newsavebox, 88
NFSS, 10
\noalign, 48
\nolinebreak, 12
\nonumber, 47, 124
\nopagebreak, 35
\normalmarginpar, 32
\normalsize, 2
\not, 45
numbering
    equations, 42, 123-125, 151
    pages, 150, 151
\numberline, 111

\oddsidemargin, 30, 31, 40, 164
\oint, 45
operators
    dot product, 54
    examples, 45
    math, 160
orphans, 35
outdenting
    in headings, 145
    page number, 151
\oval, 86
\overbrace, 44
\overline, 44

page
    blank, 35
    breaking, 38
    formatting, 164-165
    footers 32-34, 129-132
    headers 32-34, 129-132
    layout, 30
        single-column, 32
        two-column, 40
    numbering, 111, 150
    outdented number, 151
    single-column, 31
    style, 32-33

text width, 30-31, 40, 164
widows and orphans, 35
\pagebreak, 35, 41
\pagenumbering, 111
\pageref, 114
\pagestyle, 33
\paragraph, 16
paragraph
    hanging indent, 20
    indentation, 20, 146
\parbox, 18, 68
\parindent, 31, 40, 164
\parsep, 166
\parskip, 31, 40, 111, 165
\part, 16
\partopsep, 166
PBMPlus, 104
PCL files, 82-83
PCL graphics, 92-98
\phantom, 43
PICINPAR.STY, 127
PICTEX , 82, 89
picture environment, 83-88
    bezier curves, 86
    boxes, 84
    circles, 85
    example, 87
    extending, 81-82, 89
    general considerations, 81
    lines and arrows, 85
    ovals and corners, 86
    repeating objects, 87
    reusing pictures, 88
    text, 86
\pmatrix, 56
\poptabs, 62
PostScript
    files, 98
    graphics, 82-83
    tricks, 104
preamble, 105
    macros in, 107-108
preface, 109
PRINTGL, 103
\printindex, 118
\protect, 59, 116

PSFIG macros, 101
\psfig, 101-102
    options, 102
PSTricks, 104
PTIHP, 93
PTIPS, 98
\pushtabs, 62
\put, 86

quarter oval, 86-87
\qquad, 46
\quad, 46

ragged right, 15
    with hyphenation, 15
    without hyphenation, 15
\raggedright, 15
\raisebox, 18-19
raising text, 18-19
\ref, 46, 114
references, 113-114
    (see also citations)
    with superscripts, 155
relation symbols, 160
\renewcommand, 12, 107, 140, 163
\resversemarginpar, 32
reusing pictures, 88
\right, 49
\rightline, 19
\rightmargin, 166
\rightmark, 34, 146
\rm, 2
roman numerals, 36, 111
root file, 105
    example, 106
\rule, 49, 65, 84
    in arrays, 152

\samepage, 35
sans serif, 2, 144
\savebox, 88
\scriptscriptstyle, 50
\scriptsize, 2
\scriptstyle, 50
secnumdepth, 16, 165
section levels, 164
section titles, with math, 59

\section, 16
\setcounter, 35, 36, 163
\setlength, 30, 163
\setpcl, 94
\sf, 2
\shortstack, 86-87
side-by-side displays, 142-143
\sl, 2
slanted typestyle, 2
\sloppy, 12, 14
small capitals, 2
\small, 2
\smash, 67
smiley faces, 9-10
spacing
    for punctuation, 11
    horizontal, 17, 46
    in eqnarray, 152
    in tables, 73-74
    italics correction, 11
    lock space, 12
    vertical, 17
special characters, 1
special symbols
    math mode, 160-161
    text mode, 1
\special, 83, 92
splines, 86
striking out, 143
\strut, 17
struts, 17, 49, 51-52, 65
style files
    adding to document, 34
    bezier, 86
    EQUATION, 123-125
    FANCYBOX, 133-134
    FANCYHDS, 129-132
    finding, 120
    HANGCAPTION, 122-123
    loading, 108
    MULTICOLS, 135-137
    PICINPAR, 127
    VERBFILE, 121
    WRAPFIG, 126
style, document
    empty, 32

first page, 33
headings, 32
myheadings, 32
plain, 32
two-column, 39-41
fonts, 2
makeidx, 118
subequations, 125
\subparagraph, 16
subscripts, examples, 43
\subsection, 16
\subsubsection, 16
superscripts
    examples, 43
    for references, 155
\symbol, 6
symbols
    math mode, 160-161
    stretching, examples, 44
    text mode, 1

tabbing, 61-64
    commands, 62
    example, 63
    versus **tabular**, 63
\tabcolsep, 74, 169
TABLE , data commands, 78-79
    example, 75
    format codes, 76-77
    macros, 74-79, 58
    prologue commands, 76
table of contents, 17
    adding entry, 110
    box for page number, 111-112
    controlling entries, 110
    creating, 109-110
    dots in, 111
    optional entry, 110
\tableofcontents, 109-110
tables
    caption, 61
    changing width, 74
    decimal alignment, 67
    fixed, 60
    floating, 37, 60
      example, 68

footnotes in, 69-70
heading alignment, 67
in **minipage**, 69-73
side-by-side, 71-73
spacing in, 73-74
to box text, 73
vertical alignment
TABLE macros, 74-79
tabular, 64-75
    commands, 65
    example, 66
    formatting, 64-65
    versus **tabbing**, 63
    formatting, 169
\teststyle, 50
TeX archives, 121
TeXCAD, 82
text
    beside graphic, 95
    boxed, 73
    height, 30
    in boxes, 18-21
    in formulas, 45
    in **picture**, 86
    indentation, 146
    keeping together, 35
    margins, 30
    multicolumn, 135
    vertical alignment, 74
    wrapped around figure, 126-128
\textfloatsep, 37, 168
\textfraction, 37, 38, 168
\textheight, 30, 31, 40, 164
\textstyle, 43
\textwidth, 30, 31, 40, 164
\thefootnote, 113
\thepage, 34
\thispagestyle, 33
\tiny, 2
title page, 109
toc, 110-111
tocdepth, 110, 165
\today, 34
\topfraction, 37, 38-39, 168
\topmargin, 30, 31, 40, 164
topnumber, 38, 167

\topsep, 166
\topskip, 165
totalnumber, 38, 168
\tt, 2
TUG, 121
two-column, 39-41
    formatting, 165-166
\twocolumn, 39
typewriter font, 2

unavailable font, 4-5
\underbrace, 44
\underline, 17, 44
underlining, 16-17, 143
\unitlength, 84
\usebox, 88
\usecounter, 26

\vector, 85
\verb, 29
verbatim from a file, 121
\verbatimfile, 121
\verbatimlisting, 121
VERBFILE.STY, 121-122
\vfill, 17
\vline, 65
\vphantom, 56
\vspace, 17

\whiledo, 142
\widowpenalty, 35
widows, 35
WRAPFIG.STY, 126

xfig, 82

\yesnumber, 48, 124